The Reader's Odyssey

AN INDIVIDUALIZED LITERATURE PROGRAM
FOR HOMESCHOOLING
MIDDLE AND HIGH SCHOOL STUDENTS

Dena M. Luchsinger

CRECER PUBLICATIONS

WASILLA, ALASKA

Requests for permission should be addressed to:

Crecer Publications
1161 N. Iroquois Drive
Wasilla, Alaska 99654

Includes bibliographical references and index.
ISBN 978-0-9848313-1-9 (paper)

Printed in the United States of America
First edition published 2012

Dedication

This book is dedicated to my daughters and fellow readers, Kristen and Lauren.

Thank you, my dears, for sharing your journeys with me.

Table of Contents

INTRODUCTION

One begins by picking up a story and reading it
with the same wonder that one had as a child.

—*Allan Bloom*

THE GIRL WHO SAT NEXT TO ME at the awards banquet was smart. She'd taken top honors in the academic competition that had just ended, and in her bio she'd mentioned of her great love of reading classic books. So between bites of slightly overcooked chicken, I asked her which were her favorite classics.

"Um," she said, taking a bite of chicken. "*The Great Gatsby?*"

"Really?" I was surprised. It was a classic, to be sure, but I'd never heard a high school student say it was her favorite. Most young people, I think, find it hard to be very enthusiastic about a book in which the main character dies meaninglessly in the end. But, I said to myself, to each her own. I asked, "So why did you like *The Great Gatsby?*"

Clearly, no one had ever posed such a question to her before. She shoved the potatoes around on her plate and looked uncomfortable. "I don't know," the girl said. "I just do."

The girl, then a junior, reminded me of myself at that age. I'd been a book lover through elementary school, but by the time I got to high school, my love of reading had waned. I knew I'd once loved books, and I wanted to love books still, but years of being forced to read books someone else had selected for me to read, analyze, and write papers about had taken the joy out of reading. And yet, I would have answered anyone who asked me that I loved reading the classics I'd been assigned, and if anyone had asked me why, I would have looked uncomfortable, too.

Time and again, I've heard teenagers express this same ambivalence and confusion about the books they read. Some of them want to be the kind of person who loves literature, but since they can't quite manage this, they feign it. Others feel good about getting good grades and imagine that they love literature, even though they don't read such books on their own time; they too are usually just feigning. Still other students openly express disgust for literature classes. Sure, there are a few exceptional teachers out there who really get through to their students, but these by definition are rare. Most secondary students never develop a propensity for reading great literature on their own.

THE (POST)MODERN LITERARY MINEFIELD

If kids aren't too keen on literature, their parents are just plain flummoxed by the inappropriate reading content secondary students are often asked to read in school these days. Once upon a time, parents in communities formed alliances and complained when their students were asked to read inappropriate matter, but oddly enough, even as reading material has gotten more objectionable, it seems that parents bond together to complain less. Part of the reason for this may be that it is harder and harder to be heard.

Not long ago, one of my daughter's friends asked me to help her pick a required three books from the list of twenty or so that her teacher had approved for her students to read. I was astounded to see that well over half of the books on the list contained inappropriate material. Of course, high school students have no way of predicting whether a particular book is going to shock, horrify, or offend them when they pick it off a teacher's list. Such lists provide teachers a convenient defense should anyone protest a book's objectionable content: the student didn't have to choose the book he or she did. Public school literature classes have become a minefield for adolescents: few students complete high school without being exposed to rampant vulgarity, graphic rape scenes, or morally ambiguous ideals in the books they are assigned to read.

I am convinced, however, that the decrease in official protests reflects less upon decreasing interest among parents but waning social capital—that is, too many parents are overworked and spread too thin to try to generate the necessary social momentum to convince educators that many of the works of contemporary fiction students get assigned in literature classes seriously offend them. Increasingly, rather than fighting the system, parents who care about what their students are reading are removing their students from it and enrolling them in private schools or teaching them at home.

PARENTS WANT BETTER FOR THEIR KIDS

More and more, parents who take their children's moral and intellectual well-being seriously are teaching them at home, and the content in some public school literature courses is one of the best reasons to do so. Many parents and their students are disturbed—not by algebra or chemistry class, but by what some teachers are assigning students to read for literature.

Parents who elect to teach their students at home avoid some of the most disturbing aspects of what many public school literature courses now teach, but they often feel uncertain when it comes to designing a literature course that works much better. Some homeschoolers turn to ready-made literature courses or curriculums that cater to their family's values, not realizing that many of these replicate the basic flaws that create confusion and disdain in students. Others observe that their students read voluntarily on their own and see no point in meddling with what doesn't appear to be broken. Both of these approaches certainly improve upon some of the worst practices in literature courses, but neither can substantially improve upon what a typical student might achieve in a typical public school experience—and if you're going to invest the time and energy in teaching your own child, obviously, it's because you want to do better. Still other families struggle with a student who would never voluntarily choose to have anything to do with literature at all. For these families, the question of how to make literature accessible and appealing is a critical one.

It is my conviction that with a little guidance, homeschooling families can do substantially better for their kids. That is not to say that I think that all public high school teachers or programs are bad—I'm sure that many passionate and talented English teachers out there are changing lives for the better every day, and I remember my own junior and high school English teachers with fondness and gratitude. Still, English classes have changed since I was young, and not all of the changes have been for the better.

In fact, when my husband and I decided to bring our daughter home, we did not do so to protest the school she attended in any way. We did it because she was struggling, both socially and academically, and as a "twice exceptional" (gifted and talented learning disabled) student, Kristen needed an individualized program that her school, because of her passing scores on standardized testing, could not offer.

In retrospect, I'm glad we had to homeschool Kristen. Not only did I discover that I loved teaching Kristen and learning with her, but we soon decided that it would benefit our other daughter to have an individualized academic program at home as well. Individualization, I have discovered, is one of the greatest benefits a homeschooling family can offer their students. Any time a program perfectly fits a student's interests and abilities and allows students to make choices about their own learning, students will invariably be better off than with a one-size-fits-all situation or even in a small-medium-large kind of class.

So without condemning public schools outright or suggesting that this program is necessarily best for all students (a few students really do thrive in a competitive environment with more peers), I'd like to share what I have learned about designing an individualized literature program for middle and high school students that entices, challenges, and encourages students to achieve their own potential.

The program I describe is not a ready-made curriculum a parent could hand a student and walk away from, but I hope you find that you wouldn't want to. Now that Kristen has graduated and moved away, I realize that among my fondest memories from her high school years are of the discussions we had about books we were reading: pondering whether Malvolio deserved what he got and how anyone could be a fan of Falstaff. Mind you, I never liked Shakespeare in high school myself, so don't assume too quickly that literature is beyond you. I thought it was beyond me, too, until I took it up again with my daughter and learned to love it. My hope is that you as an educator will discover the joy of learning and growing with your student, too.

OUR JOURNEY FROM DRUDGERY TO PROPENSITY

I never expected to teach my daughter at home—in fact, the need to do so took me very much by surprise. So when it became clear that it was in Kristen's best interest to remove her from our local public middle school halfway through the sixth grade, I relied on what memories I had of middle and high school to guide my initial decisions as a teacher.

I was a novice in every sense of the word. Teaching Kristen and later Lauren was a learning experience for all of us. Much of what I eventually consolidated into a coherent program for my girls I came to gradually, as I learned from my experiences teaching my daughters and the resources I read, both as a graduate student of literature and education courses and as an educating parent.

My most inspired insights came from correcting my own mistakes. Although my initial efforts at teaching literature reflected the same practices I'd experienced when I was a teenager, I was probably more stringent and definitely more demanding with Kristen than my teachers had been with me. Because my daughter had always been an avid reader, I pushed her to take on more of the difficult books I imagined she was capable of. And while Kristen complied, she didn't thrive.

I couldn't help but notice that it took Kristen quite a bit longer to polish off *The Grapes of Wrath* than it took her to read the significantly longer young adult fiction books she checked out from the public library. In fact, she'd often read a stack of twenty books in her free time in about the same number of days it took her to read a single assigned book, which she did during an hour-long English period every weekday. It wasn't that she procrastinated or had a bad attitude: she just got bored. She actually kept falling asleep while trying to make it through *The Red Badge of Courage.* Having suffered through a few snoozers in my day myself, I couldn't blame her for drifting off, but I also couldn't escape the conclusion that there had to be something wrong with a literature program that was literally turning off an avid reader.

Finally, after a year of imposed drudgery, I snapped my fingers. It seemed so obvious. Kristen enjoyed reading the books she chose. Nearly everything Kristen picked out to read herself, she liked and read with zeal. What if I stocked a bookshelf with the kinds of books she ought to be reading and let her pick her own titles? The idea was so crazy, I figured it just might work.

I started collecting classics and told my husband to build me a bookshelf to put them on. At first, the bookshelf looked bare, so I got busy buying classic titles at used book and thrift stores. I also started reading books from Kristen's bookshelf myself. Up to that point, I'd made a point of pre-reading the books I assigned Kristen so that I could explain them to her properly like the English teachers I remembered from high school, but now I realized there was no way I could pre-read three hundred books and have a lecture ready for them all. I found a curriculum for an independent reading program that provided quizzes and tests for any of 250 books and told Kristen to have at it.

And Kristen took off. Instead of slogging through (or sleeping through) classic books at a snail's pace, she raced through them, almost as fast as she formerly read fluff. *The Lord of the Rings* affected her so much she decided to learn Quenyan, the imaginary language Tolkien invented for the book. Unfortunately, there wasn't much call for imaginary elf languages in the real world, so eventually Kristen transferred her new affinity for languages to Latin and used this as a bridge to studying Greco-Roman mythology. Reading was expanding her areas of interests and her tastes, and it seemed to do so pretty painlessly. I didn't have to nag her to read good books any more; she chose to read them by herself. She even brought Shakespeare's *A Midsummer Night's Dream* with her to summer camp to read during downtime.

By the end of the first semester using this approach, I became convinced that student choice was critical to the success of any literature program, yet part of Kristen's program was still off. Even though Kristen enjoyed most of the books she was reading, her scores on quizzes were inconsistent, and she hated the curriculum's essay prompts. I spent a lot of time correcting her essays and showing her why her answers were inadequate. For her part, Kristen spent a lot of time making huffy sounds.

It was something of an "A-ha" moment for me when I realized that all of the testing I was imposing on Kristen wasn't serving any real purpose. Much of it was testing her knowledge of trivia from the books she'd read, and the essays were essentially tests, checking to see if she could come up with the right answer for the prompt. Something about testing Kristen on her acquisition of correct answers didn't line up right with the ideal of loving literature and getting something unique and totally personal out of it, like the love of language and mythology Kristen had gotten from Tolkien. Freed from my prompts, Kristen wrote an essay that explored the ways that Tolkien's extensive history of Middle Earth in *The Silmarillion* enriched her reading of *The Lord of the Rings*. The insights she set forth in that essay did not answer any question I had for her, but they represented ideas that fascinated her. It was her strongest essay up to that point, by far.

The best literary analysis, we decided, comes from within. About that time, we were working through the plays of Shakespeare and had discovered that we preferred reading essays about the plays better than the instructional DVD course I'd picked out. Many of the essays we read were almost as entertaining to read as the plays themselves: "It is a little unusual," Northop Frye wrote, "for someone who has an appointment to see his mother to stop on the way and remind himself in a soliloquy that he must be careful not to murder her" (1986, p. 88). What an insight! We got the feeling that these authors loved the plays they were writing about and relished exploring them further in writing—nothing like the literary analyses I'd been assigning Kristen to test her recall and interpretative abilities. It occurred to me that what a student needs in order to think deeper about literature is not testing, but a conversation partner and a few key terms, maybe a few insights about how to understand and interpret literature. For the last two years of her program, all of Kristen's essays were topics that came up in conversations that Kristen wanted to explore more thoroughly in writing.

The decision to drop the testing aspect of our program was scary nevertheless. The quizzes and tests came from a Real Curriculum, so they were a comfort to me—they made me feel like I was teaching my daughter Real Literature. Dropping them was a very real departure from the security of working from something legitimate. And yet, I found support for my ideas in the writings of educational philosophers like John Dewey and Maria Montessori, both of whom affirmed the principle of guided independence in education. I found much to admire also in the theories of Mortimer Adler, whose *Paideia Proposal* emphasized the acquisition of increasingly complex levels of skill in reading and writing through guided practice and increasingly sophisticated understanding through the discussion of great books (1982, p. 22, 23). All of these helped me to feel confident about and embrace our home-grown literature course.

Happily, we found that ditching the curriculum didn't seem to hurt; in fact, it helped. I found myself appreciating anew the principles I'd learned back in college as a student of biblical hermeneutics. We engaged with the books we were reading, deriving meaning from the structural unity of books, and we enjoyed lively discussions about the books we had both read. Believe it or not, we actually began to look forward to the prospect of writing a particular literary analysis that suddenly seemed like an opportunity to think an idea through, rather than a chore that had to be done.

And the strange new strategy seems to work: my youngest daughter Lauren, currently in 7th grade, relishes choosing her books and impressing me by exceeding the few requirements I give her. In fact, one quarter into this school year, she's already polished off works by Isaac Asimov, Jack London, Charles Dickens, Arthur Conan Doyle, Felix Salten, and Oscar Wilde. She recently commented that the two contemporary books she read for "fun" were actually not as good as the classics. Fancy that: a twelve-year-old developing taste. Kristen, who'd earned a D in her public middle school language arts class just five years before, wound up earning a perfect score on the reading section of the SAT college entrance exam. Today, she studies at St. John's College in Annapolis, where she continues to read and discuss literature in the school's Great Book focused liberal arts program—and she is loving every minute of it.

WHY THIS BOOK

As our enthusiasm for language arts became known, a few friends and families in our homeschooling community began looking to me for advice. Some of these parents have struggled especially with students who dislike reading altogether, and it has been principally for them that I have facilitated classes and led workshops to share what I've learned. The parents who came to me wanted their students not only to do literature but to love it. Like me, they want the best for their students, but they're just not sure how to go about it. It's scary to be responsible for something so important as one's own child's education. I get that. I've been there. I was terrified that I would fail as Kristen's teacher. And yet, parents of students who are slowly learning to hate literature know that something's got to change. They want more than anything to help their students engage with literature and learn to love it. In a very real way, I wrote this book for these parents. Because I've seen my daughter go from stagnated and depressed to contented and growing, I want other people to see the same qualities emerge in their students, too. It is a wonderful thing to see your own child thrive.

Of course, much of my advice is really very simple: have clear goals and requirements, give students as much freedom and encouragement as possible, individualize content and processes, and treat students with respect. Then again, much of what I have to say is confusing, in large part because I don't really approach literature quite the way I'm supposed to, and I don't do everything the state content standards say

I should. I've decided, somewhat belligerently, that I don't care what the experts (well, some of the experts, anyway) say. I only do what works.

I'm going to suggest that the role of a teacher is to organize work, entice students to engage, and then (and this is the hard part) trust their students to make good choices. Students who are enticed by books that are appealing but challenging grow naturally, and they voluntarily choose increasingly sophisticated literary works. I also suggest that the most efficient program eliminates testing and focuses on teaching, providing students opportunities to practice reading and classifying books first, and interpreting, analyzing, and evaluating them only later. Unlike programs that measure progress by collecting scores from unrelated quizzes, essays, and tests, I suggest parents simply compare, on an annual or semi-annual basis, the quality of literature students independently elect and the quality of response students are capable of producing. Finally, I am going to suggest that the best part of any homeschool literature program is the opportunity for parents to interact with their students and to offer feedback that doesn't belittle but rather respects students as readers and as growing appreciators of good and beautiful ideas.

Although throughout most of this book I refer to this as a program for high school students, in fact, there is no reason it wouldn't apply to middle school students in the same way. Simply spread the stages of the program out over whatever timeframe you're looking at, and let your student progress to the next stage when he or she is ready—which is actually the same advice I would give parents who are considering this program for their high school students. Far better to have a high school student have experienced and loved a few great books but never to have analyzed even one than to have analyzed twenty literary works but never to have loved even one of them.

About half of this book describes the rationale for this program. Chapter I clarifies the outcomes this program seeks for students as well as how these differ from those in public school programs, which comply with national and state content standards. Chapter II asserts that allowing students choice over reading material is the key to students actually appreciating literature—and possibly eliminating some behavioral defects as well. Chapter III focuses on your job, which is organizing work for the student, and Chapter IV offers advice for individualizing the program to challenge all students wherever they are at academically, without discouraging them. Finally, Chapter V shows you how to evaluate progress without resorting to annoying testing or subjective grading. The second half of the book contains several appendices which offer practical tools such as templates for reading logs and learning contracts, samples of and lessons for various written responses to reading literature, checklists and worksheets that teach literary terms and interpretation, and resources to help you select appropriate literature for your student's program.

If you want your student to engage with good and great books, really love them, and be able to answer someone when they ask what about the books they're reading is worth loving, then consider the program that has worked for me. This book was written for dedicated parents like you—parents who know they can do better.

CHAPTER I
LITERATURE COURSE OUTCOMES

Every child should be able to look forward not only to growing up
but also to continued growth in all human dimensions throughout life.
—*Mortimer Adler*

THE CHALLENGE:

What are the goals of a high school literature program, and how can parents with limited experience with literature develop a program that addresses all of the outcomes students are supposed to achieve in high school?

If you've ever practiced archery, you know that you have to aim if you want to hit the target. Personally, I'm not that good at archery. Even when I try my hardest, a lot of my arrows miss and go back into the woods. In my defense, archery is not that simple! You have to master a particular way of holding the bow and arrow. You need brute strength to pull the arrow back and keep it there until you've corrected your aim. You need to hold the bow steady, even though your muscles, strained to maximum capacity, are shaking. That's what makes archery challenging, and it's the challenge that makes it so exciting when you actually hit the target. But if there's one thing I've learned from practicing archery, it's this: if you don't aim at the bull's-eye, you're very unlikely to hit it.

SPECIFYING DESIRED OUTCOMES

When it comes to education, you have to know what you're aiming at if you want to hit it. What exactly is the point of reading fiction and non-fiction, poetry and plays? Unless you have some idea of what purpose you want to attain with your language arts program, you're not likely to attain it, at least not with any degree of precision.

Designing a course with specific outcomes in mind is how professional teachers are trained to think, but since most states now employ content standards that tell them what they have to cover in a given year, most teachers have their hands tied. They can't really design their instruction for long-term outcomes because they have to cover the short-term goals that'll show up on standardized testing. Most public school teachers have limited freedom to think about what goals they're trying to achieve with a class; they more or less have to go through the motions and hope their students perform.

When I look at the state mandated standards that govern outcomes in Alaska's public schools, I can see why so many public high school students aren't getting much out of their English and language arts programs. Our Content Standards identify five broad outcomes for English and Language Arts as well as a list of items that describe what a successful student should be able to do. Successful students, it seems, demonstrate success in language arts not only by reading, writing, and speaking well, but by engaging in such far-ranging applications as using various tools of technology, evaluating movies, reflecting on and analyzing art, role playing, recognizing the communication styles of different cultures, and, "when appropriate," miming (Alaska, 1995).

There's a lot going on in English class these days! So much, in fact, that many students aren't mastering the essentials. With so much to do, they're just not getting the time and attention they need to truly develop the propensity for lifelong enrichment a literature course is supposed to teach. Instead, many if not most literature courses get sidetracked by what should be a subsidiary effect of a strong program: the derivation of specific personal and cultural values from teacher-selected books.

As a homeschooling parent, you have considerably more freedom to define what outcomes you want to see your student achieve. One of the advantages you have is that you don't have to cover everything public school teachers have to, and that's key: the more precisely you can define the long-term outcomes you want to see your student develop over the course of four years, the more likely your student will achieve them.

Two Objectives, One Outcome

A basic principle for solid instruction is that "an educational program is not effective if so much is attempted that little is accomplished" (Tyler, 1949, p. 33). Focus on outcomes that will serve your student throughout life. You have the unique opportunity among educators to be clear about what you want your student to achieve, and you can design a clear, consistent program that focuses on fewer goals so that your student can absolutely achieve them.

So what outcomes should students accomplish by participating in and completing a high school literature course? Ralph Tyler, formerly a Professor of Education and author of the seminal text, *Basic Principles of Curriculum and Instruction*, wrote that the purpose of education is "to broaden and deepen the student's interest so that he will continue his education long after he has ended his formal school training" (1949, p. 11). Tyler's wording is concise and clear, and his point is applicable here: a literature course should give your student greater breadth—as in variety of interests and tastes— and greater depth—as in understanding literary works of increasing level of difficulty. It should train students to read and think more broadly and better about more sophisticated ideas than they do now.

This dual focus on 'breadth and depth' captures the essence of the language used in the Standards for the English Language Arts, which are jointly determined by the National Council of Teachers of English and the International Reading Association. These emphasize the importance of breadth: "Students read a wide range of . . . fiction and nonfiction, classic and contemporary works" as well as depth: "to build an understanding . . . to acquire new information . . . to comprehend, interpret, evaluate, and appreciate" (NCTE/IRA Standards).

As you will see, both of these outcomes can be achieved through a well-designed, cohesive four-year literature program, and certainly, increasing literary breadth and depth are adequate outcomes for any literature program. The difficulty many literature programs have is that they fail to recognize that breadth and depth are means, not ends. A program that forces students to read and report on reading in order to earn a grade but fails to instill in students the innate desire to look to books to get information they need, to provide a pleasurable pastime, or to enrich their lives with challenging questions and perspectives ultimately has accomplished very little.

The real end of any course of education is to develop in students a propensity to continue to learn and grow even after no one makes them do so. Without this propensity, people stagnate intellectually, professionally, and personally. Therefore, not only breadth and depth, but specifically the propensity to read with breadth and depth must be the clear outcome sought by any high school literature program if it is to be considered successful.

The development of a propensity in students to feed their minds with what is truly good is the main goal and outcome for the program described in this book. Unfortunately, many literature courses and curriculums do the very opposite: they teach students to dislike the good (and the not-so-good) books that are imposed upon them, materially depriving students of one of life's great pleasures and purveyors of personal growth. Obviously, that is not because other programs are trying to deprive students— on the contrary, most serious literature programs attempt to help students learn to love literature as passionately as its creators.

COMPETENT READERS, NOT SPECIALISTS

Part of the flaw in the current system is that the good folks who make most state content standards and the literature courses that meet them are experts: they're people who have dedicated their lives to specializing in English literature. You'd think that was a good thing, but actually, it's not. Because when the specialists who design content standards and curriculums decided what was meant by a successful English student, what they pictured was themselves.

A few years ago, I picked up a book written by an English teacher to teach young people to interpret literature. Since my daughter was then in high school, I figured I would have her read it. But after I read the book, I wasn't convinced. It insinuated that interpreting literature was mostly about catching embedded allusions and symbolism. And while it's true that readers familiar with the Bible, mythology, and Shakespeare typically do get more out of literature than those who aren't, the recommendation to constantly be seeking symbols stuck me as misguided or at least overstated. Constantly being on the lookout for symbols denies readers the possibility of losing themselves in a great story; it turns reading into a huge and frustrating exercise, a less fun, all-words version of *Where's Waldo.* (And *Where's Waldo* was never all that fun in the first place.)

For the most part, symbolism embellishes the meaning that, in most literature, is conveyed primarily through a work's plot and character development. True, some of the best authors infuse their works with symbolic actions and objects representing abstractions: Tolkien's One Ring and Rowling's Elder Wand and Lucas' Light Saber all obviously symbolize power. But these authors use symbols in fairly unambiguous ways; the general reader doesn't need an expert to point them out. Nor is it a mystery to grasp the effect they are supposed to have upon the reader. Of course, if the symbolism in a work intrigued a student, there's no reason why he or she shouldn't explore it further—but symbolism is just one of many aspects of a work that might intrigue a reader.

In contrast, literary critics seem to relish seeking out more ambiguous symbolism in literature that is neither necessary to the general reader nor particularly obvious to anyone. For instance, in the introductory notes to a recent edition of Elizabeth Gaskell's *North and South*, Patricia Ingham suggests that the character Thornton observes the protagonist's loose bracelet slipping down her arm as she prepares tea as "a glimpse of her sexuality and its delights" (cited in Gaskell, p. xv). Now, Ingham might be right about this—certainly, she's the expert, and I did find most of her commentary quite helpful—but that particular scene I read differently. I believe Gaskell wrote the scene to depict Thornton's fascination with his friend's daughter as so great that even her loose bracelet slipping down distracts him from conversation with her father. That's charming. But Ingham's Thornton, a man who sees in his mentor's young daughter "a glimpse of sexual delights," to me, is distinctly creepy. It would absolutely disturb me to know that one of my husband's friends came over, ostentatiously to chat with my husband, but in reality to surreptitiously ogle one of my teenaged daughters. For me, the suggested symbolic meaning in that detail changes Thornton's character, and for me, not for the better. The way I see it, experts enjoy finding these little gems hidden in the literature they read—and that's wonderful for them—but for me and perhaps for most readers, it's just as well to take literature at face value.

The notion that great books could never be taken at face value was precisely one of the chief factors in turning me off of reading when I was in high school. It took me several years to get over thinking that classic literature was too highbrow for common people like me when in fact, the Austens and Gaskells, the Dickens and Twains all wrote primarily for the reading public—not just for literary critics. Their books were meant to be read and enjoyed; they were meant also to enrich and instruct their readers. There is no reason people today can't enjoy them in the same way.

The underlying philosophy for this program differs from that of most literature programs in that it rejects the notion that successful high school students should read like specialists. Those that do enjoy such close reading of literature can and should specialize in college—because appropriately, college is where students specialize, not in high school. Not only are there insufficient jobs for everyone to be literary critics, most people just plain don't like reading with that kind of depth and intensity. In fact, training students to read at the depth and intensity of a specialist at the expense of liking literature at all prevents most high school students from developing the propensity to seek out literature independently and find in it the kind of depth of understanding that can help them cope with life's pain, learn from the insights of others, and grow as individuals.

OPEN-MINDEDNESS VERSUS DISCERNMENT

Still another flaw with many literature programs these days is that they attempt too much. An objective you'll find listed on most state content standards is the one that says students are to appreciate and understand cultural diversity. There are a number of problems with this objective. Not only does this objective force programs to diversify instruction to accommodate this additional goal, the objective itself is difficult if not impossible to objectively measure. The only way to test whether students appreciate and understand diverse cultures and their values is to know which of the many diverse cultural values students have been taught. Any test, therefore, almost certainly must be devised by the teacher who assigned a particular book and then told the students what cultural values they were supposed to understand and appreciate as a result of reading it.

What you end up getting is a process by which students learn to adopt and express their teachers' values and interpretations in order to demonstrate cultural understanding on any tests or essays they are assigned. Students who disagree with the values set forth by the teacher's book selections or interpretations face an uncomfortable dilemma: openly dissent and risk a poor grade for failing to understand and appreciate values rightly, or quietly submit, and compromise their integrity by pretending to agree with what they believe is wrong for the sake of the good opinion of a teacher they cannot really respect. Such a situation is discomfiting and discouraging, and no sane student would wish to continue such an education.

Equally disturbing is the underlying philosophy of education that convinces public school teachers that it is their job to teach students values in the first place. Bear in mind that students are hardly blank slates by the time they reach this age; they already have values, and in many cases these have been purposefully instilled in them by their parents. So when educators determine to teach students values, what they're really doing is either reinforcing a student's values or attempting to replace them. The odds of students encountering only teachers who reinforce their family's set of values, however, are slim. Indeed, most new teaching candidates today are instructed to teach students to "open-mindedly embrace ideas, experiences, and texts that might seem strange . . . [and] off-putting" (Wiggins and McTighe, 2005, p. 99). Today's students, it seems, must all "learn how yesterday's weird idea can be commonplace today" (Wiggins and McTighe, p. 166). That's not teaching students to appreciate literature because good books are personally enriching, it's systematically debunking them of their own values in favor of a new set of values preferred by someone else—someone whose values are "weird."

This flies in the face of what should be the ultimate outcome of any consistent literature course: students who have learned to discern and engage specifically with books that are good and beautiful and true. How can literature that is "strange" and "off-putting" achieve this? How can "off-putting" literature engage students? How can "strange" literature help students relate to the characters in the books they read? As a homeschooler, you don't have to seek out weird books to challenge your student to rethink his or her values, and when you consider the negative effects of doing so, it seems clear that there is a better way to address this content standard: let it take care of itself. A literature program that teaches students to read with breadth and depth will naturally expose students to writing by authors from different cultural backgrounds expressing a variety of worthy values that need not be strange or off-putting.

When an author writes in a strange and off-putting manner, students naturally feel confused and disgusted. When an author writes beautifully and truthfully, students relate easily to the ideas in them, are affected by them, and consequently develop greater intellectual capacity, character, and integrity. Students who have been taught to read well know that good readers do not feel compelled to waste their time with poorly considered or badly expressed ideas, and when they do stumble across such writing, they stop reading and find something better. That is what a good literature program should achieve: students who can discern which books are good and great and who willingly choose to read them.

DEVELOPING PROPENSITY NATURALLY

A final distinction with this program is that it takes a developmental approach. Rather than expecting students to achieve a mature understanding of literature as a reader all at once, this literature program allows students to grow and appreciate literature with greater depth a little more with each high school year. It focuses first on encouraging students to read broadly, experimenting with a variety of genres from a variety of authors and historical periods. It does not expect students to interpret literature competently at this point but rather focuses on teaching students how structural elements reveal meaning in works of fiction. Only after becoming familiar with those structural elements and their importance for deriving meaning do students graduate to more difficult aspects of literary interpretation, analysis, and evaluation that apply to the more challenging literature students read in the junior and senior years.

This is different from most programs. In the vast majority of literature programs, lessons specifically show students how a particular work of literature should be understood: instruction comes from a teacher or from a curriculum. In this program, students learn through experience, discovering principles for interpretation and evaluation by seeing patterns emerge in their own reading. Although students may not cover all of the objectives that students would cover in another more comprehensive literature program, students are more likely to retain the principles they do uncover. And, because students who are vested in their reading read more and better than students who aren't, they are actually likely to ultimately get a great deal more out of their literature program than students who might cover more but could care less.

To go back to the archery analogy, when you have multiple targets, you can't hit them all. Programs that attempt to prioritize reading literature as specialists, embracing alternative perspectives and values, and covering every conceivable analytical insight into literature miss the mark simply because there isn't one, there are myriad. Students either hit one or miss them all. In this book, the desired outcome is clear and specific: students develop a propensity to read great books.

Keep your eye on that mark. Stay focused. Your student will be that much more likely to achieve success.

CHAPTER II
STUDENT CHOICE

If we want our students to grow to appreciate literature,
we need to give them a say in decisions about the literature they will read.
—*Nancie Atwell*

THE CHALLENGE:

How can teachers help students develop a propensity to read good and great books? What can parents do about students who lack enthusiasm or initiative to read independently? How does an educator ensure student growth?

Remember when everyone in the ninth grade had to read *Great Expectations* whether they wanted to or not? It's still that way in a lot of schools: teachers pick books and kids read them, learn what their teacher wants them to get out of them, and write essays reflecting their teacher's lectures. Homeschool students, of course, might not get the lectures, but a lot of pre-packaged literature courses work essentially the same way. I call this the "Sucking the Life out of Literature" approach to language arts, and sadly, it's what most high school students still face one way or another.

Homeschooling offers families the freedom to design an individualized language arts program, but many parents feel uncertain when it comes time to put one together. They know they don't have the expertise of a high school English teacher, and many of them turn to a pre-packaged language curriculum that prescribes a sequence of books or excerpts for students to read, analyze, write about, and be tested on. Unfortunately, homeschoolers who turn to such packages miss out on a terrific opportunity.

RESPECTING STUDENTS' PSYCHOLOGICAL NEEDS

Language arts can be the bane of any high school student's experience, but it can also be its boon. In fact, a good language arts program can turn a reluctant reader into an avid one, and the key to this amazing transformation isn't rocket science—it's actually just plain common sense. You don't even need any special expertise to implement an outstanding English program. Simply set a few parameters for the program that you and your student can agree on, and let your student decide what to read and when to read it. Homeschooling families who prioritize student choice in determining literature selections turn out more sophisticated, balanced, and advanced readers because such a language arts program honors the student's basic psychological need for freedom and fun, resolves character defects by engaging the student's whole personality, and strengthens family ties and values by encouraging meaningful discourse.

Author and pioneering English teacher Nancie Atwell (1998) found that student choice "has a major impact on students' fluency, reading rate, and comprehension" (p. 37). Designing her classroom to give her students a say about what books they would read, Atwell found that even one positive reading experience could help a reluctant reader change his or her attitude about reading, even reading the books they'd been assigned in the past and disliked: "I could never get into [*The Prince and the Pauper* and *The Call of the Wild*] because we HAD to read them," one student wrote. Later, freed to pick her own books, the same student discovered *The Call of the Wild* on her own and liked it (p. 37). The freedom to choose made all the difference.

The reason this approach gets even struggling readers motivated to read faster and better is that it respects students' need for freedom and fun. It might not surprise you to know that students perform better when they can choose to do as they like, but that freedom and fun are actually psychological needs might. Educational psychologist Glasser (1988) identifies four psychological needs that determine the way people behave: that of belonging and feeling loved and included in a group, that of having the power to exert one's will effectively, that of being free to think and act on one's own opinions and preferences, and that of having fun and seeking a reprieve from boredom through activities that are enjoyable or amusing (p. 25 – 30). Glasser points out that, once basic physical needs are met, people always choose behaviors that satisfy one or more of these four psychological needs (p. 21). In particular, they will act in response to the need they feel most deprived of. People who are bored, for instance, seek out something intriguing or fun. People who feel restrained seek out freedom. People who feel oppressed try to do whatever they can to get a little more power. And people who feel excluded seek friends (p. 15).

Glasser's observations hold important implications for students of literature because students who perceive assigned reading to be boring are unlikely to engage with it or give it their full attention. Because they are bored, their eyes and ears will be easily distracted and their minds will be constantly prone to being diverted by more interesting ideas. If they have any opportunity at all, they'll drop the book and get busy putting those more interesting ideas into action.

ACKNOWLEDGING STUDENTS' PERSPECTIVES

But there's something else at going on here. Because the issue is not entirely that the book is boring, is it? It's the *perception* that the book is boring that affects students. When teachers assign books, most students automatically assume that the book is not something they would have chosen for themselves—and since they *didn't* choose it, they reason that given the choice, they probably *wouldn't*. By high school, students know from past experiences that they enjoyed the books that they picked out for themselves much more than the books that they'd been assigned to read. Of course, most students conveniently forget about the books they chose and then gave up on because they weren't as good as they looked, but then again, assigned reading never comes with the option of ditching a book that proves to be dull. The perception of assigned reading being boring becomes a self-fulfilling prophecy, since people "tend to perceive and think about others and situations in terms of the ideas we have already formed about them" (Kirby, Goodpaster, & Levin, 2001, p. 27).

These perceptions may or may not be accurate, but they definitely affect they way people experience reality. Even students who like reading tend to have a better perception of books they've chosen themselves. My daughter is a good example here. She always loved reading and her reading scores had always been high. But when I started homeschooling her, I made the mistake of assigning books for her to read. I didn't want her to bog down in easy or fun reading selections. If you want to know the truth, I didn't trust her to make good choices.

So I made bad choices for her instead. The first year I homeschooled Kristen, I made her read *The Great Gatsby*, *The Grapes of Wrath*, *The Lord of the Flies*, and *The Red Badge of Courage*. She read them for me, but she didn't like even one of them. Then, about halfway through the school year, she asked if she could read *The Iliad* instead of whatever title I'd picked out for her to read next. She said she had enjoyed what little she'd learned about mythology in elementary school and wanted to read "the real thing." So I agreed. How can you not let your kid read one of the most challenging titles in all of literature if she asks for it? I didn't think she'd finish, but much to my surprise, she stuck with it. Although it took her a couple of months to make it through all 496 pages, she claimed to have liked *The Iliad* more than all the other books I'd made her read. Having the freedom to choose makes that much difference.

Why should students read *Moby Dick* if they don't like it? The only reason they have to read *Moby Dick* is because someone else has arbitrarily inflicted it upon them and made their grade dependent upon their compliance. Students know perfectly well that any one of a hundred other books would have done just as well for meeting whatever state standards or college admission requirements the teacher is attempting to meet. The assignment feels oppressive, and people who feel oppressed often seek out some way to rebel. In fact, imposing an arbitrarily imposed agenda on students, far from helping them grow, actually results in students developing so many of the negative character traits that get so much attention and waste so much time in schools today.

ADDRESSING DEFECTIVE CHARACTER TRAITS

The most obviously negative character trait Montessori (1967) calls the "strong" character: students who resist authority and sometimes use aggressive or even violent behaviors to overcome obstacles. These students are disobedient, possessive, noisy, and "often unkind;" Montessori also notes that "strong" students often seem to lack the ability to focus or concentrate, coordinate fine-motor tasks, or organize their thoughts (p. 197). Another defective character is "weak." This type of student tends not to demonstrate obvious problem behaviors—in fact, they often appear to be good and obedient. The defect is that they tend to be clingy, whiny, overly sensitive, and "easily bored" (p. 197, 198). Still a third character type Montessori seems to find annoying: "those thought to be superior . . . [whose] company is none too agreeable" (p. 201).

Here's the interesting bit: what Montessori and her colleagues found was that all of these "defective" character traits disappeared when students engaged in purposeful activity of the student's own choosing (p. 202). This "normalization [of the various negative character types] comes through concentration on a piece of work" (p. 206). Even the most seemingly hyperactive, distracted, or lethargic children seem like different people altogether when a task engages their concentration. Montessori writes, "An interesting piece of work, freely chosen, which has the virtue of inducing concentration rather than fatigue, adds to the child's energies and mental capacities, and leads him to self-mastery" (p. 207).

ASSURING PROGRESS AND GROWTH

But it is not enough for students to be well-adjusted and engaged in reading: education implies progress and growth. Without some direction, most students soon plateau, choosing only books that entertain them most. How can teachers entice students to voluntarily choose increasingly difficult reading matter of their own accord?

Most literature programs prescribe readings in order to teach objectives in a specific order or in support of a specific framework. These programs generally order objectives so that students tackle the simplest texts first and more difficult works last. For students following this type of curriculum, whether in a public schools or home-based program, stagnation is not really an option because the growth is built-in. The only problem with this guaranteed growth is that it comes at the price of student choice, and, for many students, at the price of developing a taste for the type of growth-producing reading in the future as well—a catch-22 something like those diets that produce amazing results that disappear the instant the dieter stops following the prescribed Spartan regime.

A framework that I pondered for some time is the one proposed in Jessie Wise and Susan Wise Bauer's *The Well-Trained Mind.* That framework, based on a philosophy of classical education, advises students to choose literary works from fairly extensive lists reflecting four distinct historical periods. The difficulty with the framework, at least for us, was that the chronology had freshmen reading ancient poems, dramas and philosophy first, sophomores reading medieval theology and philosophy next, juniors reading Renaissance and Reformation works after that, and seniors reading modern literature and novels last. The order of readings seemed to put the hardest reading first, and the easiest last (not that the easiest readings are all that easy).

Now, if a student were motivated to take on that kind of grueling literature program, fantastic—but it would take an exceptional student to do so. Most students at the middle and high school levels are still accumulating experience with books and gaining confidence and ambition, working toward that point where an extremely difficult book seems more like an exciting challenge rather than a hideous chore.

So the question becomes how to balance allowing students the freedom to choose their own reading with the necessity of requiring students to tackle literature projects that constitute increasing levels of challenge. One answer comes from the philosophy of educational theorist John Dewey:

> [The educator] must survey the capacities and needs of the particular set of individuals with whom he is dealing and must at the same time arrange the conditions which provide the subject-matter or content for experiences that satisfy these needs and develop these capacities. The planning must be flexible enough for permit free play for individuality of experience and yet firm enough to give direction towards continuous development of power. (1938, p. 58)

According to Dewey, the educator's duty is to *survey capacities and needs* and to *arrange conditions*: to understand the students' abilities, interests, and tastes, and to then set up an environment that invites students to take the next step toward personal growth.

Maria Montessori (1967) agrees: "The children in our schools are free," she writes, "but that does not mean there is no organization. Organization, in fact, is necessary, and if the children are free to work, it must be even more thorough than in ordinary schools" (p. 244). This principle of being "even more thorough than ordinary schools" is essential: students freed from oppression thrive in liberty, but because they are still students, they need teachers to organize work for them. "The teacher . . . attends to [the environment] instead of being distracted by the [students'] restlessness. From this will come healing, and the attraction that captures and polarizes the [student's] will" (p. 277). Rather than fixating on students and distracting them with constant nagging, criticism, and praise, Montessori's teachers concentrate on organizing enticing work for the students. In other words, teachers model the behavior they wish to see students emulate: that of engaging with a meaningful task.

Work, incidentally, in Montessori's world, refers not to pointless drudgery or busy work, but to engaging tasks that students lose themselves in, like organizing one's own possessions, building a sand castle, painting a picture, performing an experiment just to see what happens, climbing a tree, reading a really good book, or striving to reach a goal one has set for oneself: it refers to engagement.

Montessori, whose initial experiments in education involved mentally retarded students, believed that all students could be engaged by meaningful tasks—and my experiences with developmentally disabled and autistic students lead me to agree. All students can and will engage in serious tasks so long as the tasks provided are meaningful to them in some way.

ENTICING STUDENTS TO BEGIN A PERSONAL ODYSSEY

Students who have not yet learned the value of engaging in reading must be enticed, at least initially. This is, for Montessori, the second phase of work (p. 278). How do you convince students to engage? Montessori uses the illustration of a teacher who says, "Let's move all the furniture today!" and enthusiastically sets to work with students. For a reluctant literature student, enticement might look more like, "Let's watch The Three Musketeers" today!" or "Let's act out this love scene from *Romeo and Juliet* with corny British accents!" or "Let's make a top ten list of the worst books ever!" This last item might seem counterproductive, but remember that evaluating books that don't work is as much the work of literature gurus as praising books that do, so don't be afraid to use wherever your student is at to draw him or her into the discussion. The main point is to engage and even to amuse—to get students to engage and get into literature in some way.

So far, teachers are to organize work and entice students—which most teachers attempt to do in one way or another—but Montessori's third challenge is both simplest and hardest for most teachers: to back off. Montessori warns teachers not to interfere with students who have begun to engage in real work. In part, this is because interference often means taking back ownership for what should be the student's project: "If the child is trying to lift something very heavy and the teacher tries to help him, it often happens that he leaves the object in her hands and runs away" (p. 280). In a literature course, the danger is to take back the student's freedom and to take over once again: the student attempts not to lift something heavy but to construct something very personal: a repertoire of reading that reflects not only his or her personal tastes, interests, and values but also in a very real way an odyssey, his or her own journey toward mature understanding.

To put this another way, students who understand themselves to be constructing their own personal journeys toward mature understanding see literature as edifying food for the journey, and they seek it out on their own. Students who understand themselves to be forced to march to a destination determined by and important only to someone else—whether or not it is for their own good—consider the excursion over the moment the commander no longer exerts control. Although students benefit from the exercise, the true rewards fall by the wayside.

FOSTERING TRUST AND COMMUNITY

So getting students to choose growth is in a very real way a matter of trust. It's no good pretending to offer freedom when in fact you retain control. Instead, you arrange the conditions that allow students to have maximum freedom—much like you arrange your home to allow toddlers freedom to explore safely—and you organize work that includes a few minimum requirements to ensure growth. Organizing work in this way satisfies students' need to be engaged, to develop their intellectual powers, and to gain admittance into a community of similarly-minded, educated readers.

It's important to remember this social, community-of-readers aspect of reading, because on first glance, reading might seem to be a primarily solitary enterprise. In fact, literature is a very social thing. Books are written by people, for people. If books are any good, they generate discussion between people. When people read ideas that excite or anger them, they want to talk about those ideas with others. When they find a book to be enriching and worthwhile, they normally recommend it to other people. And when people find humor in what they read, they want to share it with their friends so they can laugh together.

A language arts program that encourages your student to voluntarily read good books can actually strengthen your family bonds by fostering camaraderie and good discussions. You won't often get this from imposed reading—no one wants to share a book that bores them, and no one really enjoys discussing what they didn't care about in the first place. But when a student loves what he's reading, don't be surprised if he brings it to you spontaneously and tell you to "read just this part" or wants to talk about it in the car or over dinner. Think about how amazing that is: for a teenager to want you to know what he found intriguing or amusing, sad, or inspiring. Instead of resenting you as the dictator-slash-teacher, she's seeking you out to share her ideas, hopes, and dreams. How many parents of teenagers dream about that?

Books can be the glue that holds friendships together. Friendships, unlike parents and children, and unlike teachers and students, are made up of equals. Books have a way of doing that for us: they give people a level playing field, where each of us can enjoy and learn and share and recommend wonderful things to one another. Allowing students to choose the books that inspire them might be the beginning of a lifelong relationship—not of teacher and student, nor even as parent and child, but of equals and of friends.

CHAPTER III
ORGANIZING WORK

*Planning must be flexible enough to permit free play for
individuality of experience and yet firm enough to give direction
towards continuous development of power.*
—*John Dewey*

THE CHALLENGE:

How can teachers organize work that will entice students to go from reading books for entertainment to reading books for enrichment? What sort of expectations should teachers have of students over the course of four years?

Competence as a reader of literature is not so much an ability, but a propensity toward reading with breadth and depth. An effective literature program inspires in students a propensity toward reading good books for pleasure, information, and personal growth. Teachers need to understand that students develop this propensity toward reading through experience. Your role as a teacher is not to insist that certain works are worth reading and that students appreciate them—which will almost certainly prejudice students against the types of books you recommend—but to provide an environment that entices students to choose well by making appropriate literary options both appealing and accessible.

To read a book is an act of faith that the book will be worth the effort. Initially, students might be reluctant to read more difficult books, but if you design the program so that the student's early experiences with good and classic books are enjoyable—maybe they read primarily books that serve to entertain, rather than delving into the murky waters of interpretation—and attainable —maybe they read shorter works or books with relatively simple vocabulary—students learn that good books are indeed worth the effort. In this way, students learn to trust; they learn to believe that even very difficult books, if they are truly great, will pay off in the end.

The books from which your student chooses reading material create a context for this program. Whether or not your student learns to look forward to reading with increasing sophistication depends almost entirely upon whether the student finds the options available both accessible and appealing. Obviously, if you design a program with requirements but without accessible options, the program will have the effect of discouraging the student from the start. That's why I suggest that, if there is any way you can set up a library that caters to your students' tastes, interests, and abilities in your own home, you do so.

There really is no substitute for an in-house library. True, a book list that is sufficiently large to allow for student choice can provide guidance, but it doesn't allow for students picking up books, feeling their weight, checking out whether they have lots of dialogue or whether they're mostly gynormous descriptive paragraphs from here to eternity. Readers need to literally handle a book to determine whether they want to invest themselves in reading it.

A public library affords this option of handling books to students, but there are drawbacks with planning to use one for this program. First, students may not always have the time or resources to physically get to one. Second, libraries offer students so much choice as to stymie them. Even with a checklist in hand or a set of clear parameters to guide them, students might have to search several sections in order to locate an interesting sounding book on the list. Then, after all that effort, the book might not seem appealing after all. So public libraries, valuable as they are to communities as a whole, mean extra work for students, just in terms of finding good books to read.

The plentiful choices in libraries tend also to steer students toward the most obviously appealing books. In a public library, most classic works will have been in stock for several years, and their covers will often be scuffed and dated. Meanwhile, many libraries showcase new acquisitions, which usually feature trendy cover art that appeals to young readers. Although most librarians would probably admit a greater appreciation for classic works than trendy ones, public libraries tend not to be prejudiced when it comes to what books are most worthy of reading. As a result, the public library may inadvertently undermine the aims of your course by making the poorer books seem better and the better books seem worse.

STOCKING BOOKS FOR AN INDIVIDUALIZED HOME LIBRARY

Accessibility, ideally, means that the books from which you want your student to choose are available to your student at home. A home library doesn't require a huge number of books, but the collection you offer your student should genuinely allow for selection. If your library contains fifty titles and you expect your students to read thirty of them by the end of the year, that's not really allowing students to choose what they really want to read, it's just allowing them to reject what they really don't.

If you are truly allowing students the freedom to choose, they need a lot more latitude. A reasonable size for any initial collection is approximately whatever number of books your student might normally read in a school year times ten. So a student who might be expected to read thirty good books in a year would need a library of three hundred titles, while a student who is more likely to read ten should have the option of choosing from about a hundred. Because your student retains these books as options in subsequent years, your initial investment will be the largest by far. You will only need to refresh the library's stock each subsequent year by about 10 – 20%. These acquisitions reflect the student's expanding tastes and interests and increasing competence as a reader.

Yes, this will require a financial investment on your part, but it will probably be cheaper than you think. Here are a few good sources for finding great and appropriate inexpensive books for your literature course:

- **Swap meets**—if your local homeschool co-op or community doesn't have one, ask if you can sponsor one. Books, of course, are free.

- **Thrift stores** – look for stores that separate books into sections such as mysteries, science-fiction, young adult literature, and classics and peruse your student's favorite sections regularly. Some thrift stores price books at less than a dollar.

- **Rainbow Resource Center** (www.RainbowResource.com) discounts many classics—for instance, as of this writing (January 2012), you can get a new copy of a thrift edition of *The Adventures of Huckleberry Finn* for just $1.65. Add the free shipping on orders over $150, and this is probably the best place to stock up on new copies of classics. Incidentally, try to get new copies of classics if you can, rather than used ones. Unlike the books that appeal to your reader's specific tastes and interests, classic works need all the help they can get to entice students to pick them up. Old-fashioned cover images and worn, yellowed pages could dissuade your reader from picking up what could be a fantastic classic. Considering that classics are usually cheaper than contemporary works, it makes sense to budget for as many new classic works as possible.

- **Dover publications** (www.DoverPublications.com) also sell many classics for as little as $2.00; they offer free shipping on orders over $40 and often put titles on sale as well. Another good stock-up source.

- **Large, quality used bookstores** can be a good source for finding both classics in good condition and more contemporary books that cater to particular tastes and interests at a discounted price. These books probably won't be as cheap as a thrift store and are usually not in brand new condition, but a well-organized and large used bookstore is probably the best place for an organized library acquisition trip with your student. Just give your student an idea of what to look for and let him or her help pick out books for your library.

- **Amazon** (www.Amazon.com) is my source for everything else. It's where I go first (to see what's available and read reviews) and last (where I buy new books that I can't find cheaper elsewhere). Sometimes, you can get used books for as little as $4 (a penny for the book plus $3.99 for shipping); other times you can get books even cheaper (no idea how that works but great!). This is a fine option for the contemporary books that appeal to your student, but unless a book is hard to find, not the best choice for classics. Remember, the used books you get through sellers on Amazon might arrive with yellowing pages and goop on the cover, so unless you're buying new, like new, or very good condition books, reserve the used mail-order books for the titles you know will appeal to your student. It's still cheaper to get something for free at a swap meet or for a few cents at a thrift store, but all in all, Amazon facilitates the quickest route to cheap acquisition of specific titles.

APPEALING TO STUDENTS' CURRENT TASTES AND INTERESTS

Because you want to entice your student, stock the initial library with classic books that primarily appeal to your reader's tastes and interests, both at your student's current level of ability as well as at a level that your student will find somewhat challenging to read. When I first stocked our library, I took Kristen's fascination with everything involving animals into account. Not surprisingly, among the first books she chose to read from our home library were *Born Free*, *Animal Farm*, *Watership Down*, and *Never Cry Wolf*. It did not matter that some of these books were fairly difficult reading: because she was interested, she chose and read them eagerly.

I also kept her tastes in mind. Since Kristen enjoyed reading fantasy, I made sure our library included a number of both classic and contemporary titles from that genre.

These, too, Kristen quickly found and read: *Watership Down*, an anthropomorphic fantasy epic, was an excellent find on my part, as was *The Princess Bride*, a riotous romp of a fantasy that Kristen treated herself to after she finished the more difficult *Watership Down*.

In the same way, let your student's current interests, tastes, and ability guide your initial selections. If you're not sure what your student's tastes and interests are, sit down together and complete the Venn diagram graphic organizer included in Appendix A. Most students will have no trouble listing several items for each category and possibly a few that show up in both. For instance, students who like history tend also to like historical fiction, students who like science or technology tend to like science fiction, and students who like humor in general tend to like it also as a genre.

The information you gather from this exercise will help you to define the types of books you especially want for your library. The third circle in the Venn diagram represents classic works of literature. The areas of overlap between your student's tastes and interests and classic titles represent the books that will help to entice your student to try out more difficult literary works.

To give you an example, say a certain student listed mysteries and adventure stories for tastes and outdoor activities and dogs for interests. Classic titles that would overlap with the student's taste for mysteries might include books by mystery writers such as Agatha Christie, Sir Arthur Conan Doyle, and Dorothy Sayers. *The Hound of the Baskervilles* is a mystery that involves a dog, so you'd want to add it to your list. Other classic titles that feature dogs might include *Lad: A Dog, Lassie Come Home, The Call of the Wild*, and *The Incredible Journey*, most of which also involve some kind of adventure, increasing the odds of each appealing to the student on multiple levels. Other classic adventure stories include *Robinson Crusoe, The Three Musketeers, The Adventures of Tom Sawyer, Beat to Quarters*, and *Moby Dick*. Of course, works that are generally classified in other genres like *The Hobbit* or *20,000 Leagues Under the Sea* also involve lots of outdoor adventure, so these, too, will be worthy of consideration.

Eventually, you should have a fairly lengthy list of classic titles to consider stocking for your library. Those works that overlap with both your student's tastes and interests consider the most potentially appealing and works that overlap in only one area a little less so. Depending on your student's enthusiasm about reading, you might also want to consider also the length and level of difficulty of each work as you go about deciding which titles merit prioritizing for purchase. Appendix C classifies classics by difficulty to help you get a sense for which books will be most appropriate and appealing for your student.

Of course, your library should also include a selection of contemporary books, as well as works representing a number of different genres: drama and poetry, fiction and nonfiction. Since most classic nonfiction tends to be exceptionally difficult reading, I ensure the presence of both contemporary works and nonfiction ones by seeking out contemporary nonfiction that will specifically appeal to my student. I do this for a couple of reasons: first, it's important that students develop the habit of reading not only for pleasure but for information also, and nonfiction is the venue through which educated people seek information.

For some reason, most students get the impression that that nonfiction means boring. I don't know why—maybe they might associate nonfiction with textbooks?—but they do, and so most students are surprised to discover how engaging nonfiction books written for a trade (as opposed to academic) audience can be.

Enticing high school students to pick up a work of nonfiction isn't hard to do—just take advantage of your student's particular interests. It almost doesn't matter what a student is interested in; these days, nonfiction books on almost any topic are available to entice students who are leery of nonfiction: authors such as historians Stephen Ambrose and David McCullough, animal behaviorists Patricia McConnell and Temple Grandin, writers of popular sociology Malcolm Gladwell and Barbara Ehrenreich, travel writers Bill Bryson and Peter Jenkins, scientists James Gleick and Carl Sagan, modern muckrakers Eric Schlosser and Morgan Spurlock, humorists Stephen Colbert and Dave Barry and too many others to name write popular and engaging nonfiction.

Contemporary fiction that serves primarily to entertain shouldn't comprise too high a percentage of a high school literature program, but then again, there's no real reason to absolutely prohibit it, especially during the first half of the program while the student is learning structural elements. You might even involve your student in selecting a few books that are mostly just for fun. Believe it or not, the inclusion of a few purely entertaining titles can make a big difference on the way your student sees the entire literature program. A library stocked with only challenging material feels oppressive. Students need to see that they really do have choices, and the option of rewarding themselves for a difficult book with something fun, light, and easy.

A simple breakdown for this collection is one-third appealing classics, or works that cater to your student's current tastes and interests, one-third accessible classics, or works that are either relatively easy to read (at or only slightly above your student's reading ability) or

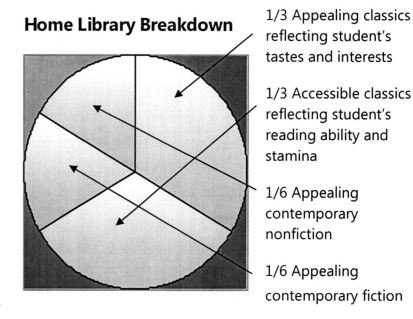

Home Library Breakdown

1/3 Appealing classics reflecting student's tastes and interests

1/3 Accessible classics reflecting student's reading ability and stamina

1/6 Appealing contemporary nonfiction

1/6 Appealing contemporary fiction

relatively short; and one-third contemporary works of primarily appealing nonfiction titles as well as a few trendy young adult fiction picks, just for fun.

ACCELERATION AND ACCUMULATION

Although you may initially have a good sense of what your student likes, you may be surprised to see how quickly those tastes and interests expand. I used Kristen's taste for fantasy to steer her toward a few more difficult authors such as Kafka and Twain. Since I knew that both of these authors had written short stories from the perspectives of animals but both were tucked away in collections of the authors' short stories where they would be hard to find, I recommended Kristen try both Kafka's "A Report to the Academy" and Twain's "A Dog's Tale." Kristen chose to give them a try and found them both delightful—again, even though neither was written with particularly easy vocabulary or style.

Prior to reading "A Dog's Life," Kristen didn't think much of Mark Twain. She had tried to read *The Adventures of Huckleberry Finn* before she was ready for it, and she thought she didn't like Mark Twain as a result. But after she read Twain's short story, she reconsidered. She read another humorous short story and was hooked. She then read both *The Prince and the Pauper* and *A Connecticut Yankee in King Arthur's Court* in rapid succession. With that, she decided she wanted to read more science fiction. Her first selection? H.G. Wells' *The Time Machine.*

This is the kind of expansion you can expect to see when you provide students with accessible and appealing options that truly entice them. When students engage with good books, you never know what associations will spring from them. The more good books students read, the more their interests expand and their tastes grow. And most exciting of all, this propensity actually accelerates as the student accumulates experience with ever broader literary experiences.

When students read difficult material, they confront new vocabulary and more complicated sentence structures. These slow readers down at first, and this discourages students if a project takes too long. But if students successfully make it through a few shorter challenging works, they learn to recognize more words and structures, making it easier to read subsequent difficult books faster.

But students don't only accumulate vocabulary, they also accumulate ideas. This accumulation of ideas works on the brain like weights on a bicep: at first, the work is hard, but as the muscle grows, it begins to crave the sensation of working and growing stronger. So the reader's mind craves more stimulation as it begins to accumulate more advanced vocabulary and ideas.

Having mastered books of an intermediate level, the brain wants to push on to more advanced material. Merely good books begin to feel inadequate to the student: the student craves more challenging ideas to chew on and ponder. The entertaining books they once enjoyed suddenly seem weak and a little empty. Eventually, such books will appeal only when the student has worked hard on a long and difficult project and needs a break.

But notice that an essential ingredient in this process is engagement: active intellectual and sometimes emotional involvement with a text. In short, students have to care in order for the ideas in a book to truly affect them. When students read literature only because they have to, they might retain material in order to pass a test, but such knowledge rarely translates into true understanding and almost never has the power to form character or inspire. Reading in this way may require exertion, but it does not force the brain to do the hard work of finding a place for new ideas in its existing schema and expanding its capacity. It is like lifting a one-pound weight: one's bicep can raise it endlessly and never begin to bulge. Students who don't engage with literature don't get stronger; and their brains, neither challenged nor growing, don't crave more. "Only the student whose mind has been engaged in thinking for itself is an active participant in the learning process that is essential to basic schooling" (Adler, 1982, p. 32).

By first building in students the propensity to engage and read a variety of books primarily for information and entertainment and then using this propensity combined with the accumulation of vocabulary and ideas to entice the student to read more challenging works with greater depth, an educator allows students to develop greater intellectual power naturally. Growth need not be imposed; it occurs as students begin to realize their own power of understanding and yearn for more. As the weightlifter senses muscular growth, he craves ever heavier weights: light weights can no longer satisfy the body's desire to increase its power. So students, sensing the power of great ideas on their intellects and characters, crave continual exercise of continually greater depth. It is a natural outcome of true engagement with great literature.

JUST ORDERING BOOKS?

So far, the teacher's work in designing this course has been mainly organizational: the gathering of information about the student's tastes, interests, and ability as well as information about the availability of reading material to both appeal and challenge the student toward growth; the decision-making about which works to acquire; and finally, the physical ordering of the environment so that students can easily peruse books.

Of course, that is not all you will do: students must know what requirements you have for them in terms of how much time to invest and how much material to cover—and these will be discussed in the next chapter—but lest you think that this input is inadequate, consider first that this organizing work is a serious, on-going task. In preparation for my daughter's literature program, I spent many hours researching what classic works might appeal to Kristen from a broad variety of diverse genres. Each subsequent year, I carefully considered what Kristen had read and what the next step might look like for her. I also talked to her about the interests she was developing, and as Kristen progressed in the program, I proposed options to her for targeting one or another literary focus.

For instance, after Kristen spent two years of sampling various types of literature, I proposed a year-long course focusing on the plays of Shakespeare. I knew that if Kristen was not interested in Shakespeare, the course would have limited value for her. As it turned out, Kristen had happened across enough references to Shakespeare in her reading that she genuinely wanted to become more familiar with more of his works. It fell to me then to organize work for her—to acquire resources for the course as well as the actual plays, both in print and on DVD. Kristen's senior year, she elected to read a few literary works in French, and again, I researched which titles would be most appropriate, given her ability in French and tastes in reading, and I stocked a few options from which she could choose. Thus the work of organizing appealing, accessible, and appropriate options is not insignificant—not at all.

THE FOUR-YEAR LITERATURE PROGRAM

How does all of this translate into a four-year course? Obviously, you want to your student to grow, so your program will build up to the most challenging literature, which comes last. Now, the most challenging texts will also occupy the most time, and toward the end of the four-year course, students should be engaging deeply in fewer literary selections.

Envision this four-year plan somewhat like a funnel that starts broad and wide and gradually narrows down to tighter focus: initially, students read a wide variety of primarily entertaining or informative works; gradually, students develop greater ability and more sophisticated interests, allowing them to commit to studying a few difficult and time-consuming works in great depth.

A basic plan for such a program looks something like this:

Freshman and Sophomore Years:

focus on breadth; entice students with appealing options to expand tastes and interests; expect students to read mainly for entertainment or information; encourage students to experiment with non-intimidating or shorter classic works that appeal to tastes and interests

Junior Year:

begin to focus on depth; expect students to take on somewhat fewer projects but for projects to represent a greater level of challenge; encourage students to delve deeper, experimenting with literature interpretation and analysis of literature as well as choosing a topic to research through nonfiction sources

Senior Year:

focus on depth: allow students to choose a nonfiction topic of interest as the focus of serious research as well as a specific focus within literature from which to engage in critical analysis and evaluation; offer students the option of choosing a 'Great Books' approach to electives such as government, philosophy, science, or ethics

As the literature course gains more focus and depth in the junior and senior years, students should have more voice about the types of books they need access to in order to focus with greater depth, especially in regard to research projects. Consider allowing your student to read nonfiction works applicable to other subjects like health, science, or social studies, and offer your student credit for the reading aspect in literature, the writing aspect in composition, and the content aspect in the corresponding subject. By allowing mature students to complete work in several subjects at once, you allow them to focus their mental energies efficiently and to produce quality work across subjects.

For instance, Kristen's senior government class involved reading, discussing, and writing about the *Constitution of the United States of America* and the *Articles of the Confederation, The Federalist, The Anti-Federalist Papers,* and *What the Anti-Federalists Stood For.* well over a thousand pages of very challenging reading. Although the course constituted significantly greater challenge than the typical textbook approach, it was Kristen's choice:

by that point in her high school career, she had become convinced that textbooks were boring and was willing to work harder to avoid using one. Because the topic was worthy—ideally, every American citizen should understand the Constitution and its implications—we decided to dedicate more time to the subject and consider various aspects of the work applicable for other courses. As I recall, Kristen completed one literature analysis and one research paper as well that semester, but the bulk of her reading efforts went toward the government course.

Such a plan allows a student to hone useful skills while emphasizing the importance of reading as a lifelong source of pleasure and enrichment. There is a sense of growth and building upon what has gone before. Each year, the student gets practice reading the same sorts of fiction and nonfiction, but at slightly more challenging levels; each year the student reinforces and multiplies ideas by reading different books on similar topics. By the end of the literature program, your student will have built a repertoire of vocabulary and ideas, familiarity with classic literature, and a genuine propensity to learn and grow.

Chapter IV
Minimizing Requirements

Choice and execution are the prerogatives and conquests of a liberated soul.
—Maria Montessori

The Challenge:

How do teachers ensure students achieve outcomes while permitting students so much freedom? What can teachers do to help students who read slowly or poorly to accomplish literature course outcomes?

In my experiences facilitating adolescent discussions, there are two ways to shut down a teenager: set the bar too high, and set the bar too low. Questions that expect students to understand too much usually go unanswered, since no one wants to hazard a guess that turns out to be wrong. But questions that are too easy are just as bad: the whole group clams up, everyone realizing that the answer is obvious and that whoever answers such a question is just a little too eager. I've learned that, as a facilitator, if I want teenagers to engage, it's best to keep things at a moderate level of challenge.

The same principle applies here. A teacher who designs a literature program that expects little or nothing of students will likely see those expectations met. Whether students do well in a course where teachers expect too much depends largely on the demeanor of each individual student—students who want to please their teacher or feel superior to other students generally do well, while others resent the teacher and the course. But teachers who design literature programs that require only the bare minimum of students and allow them the freedom to exceed the course requirements if they so choose may be surprised by the degree to which students surpass their expectations. The reasons for this are simple: students who feel trusted tend to exceed requirements, and students who feel respected tend to excel.

It sounds unlikely, but in fact, this is how the best college professors work. According to Ken Bain (2004), among successful college instructors, "requirements are pared to the bone and stem from a contract" (p. 139). Requiring the least from students in order to successfully pass the literature course might sound like a recipe for mediocrity, but actually, it's not—because these minimum requirements are paired with high expectations. A course requirement is what students must complete in order to pass the course, not necessarily what the teacher expects they are capable of completing. In fact, setting few requirements doesn't imply low expectations; rather, it suggests that the teacher trusts students to choose well, to take responsibility for their own learning, and to live up to their own potential.

And this is important for students to understand: students need to understand not only that they are being trusted to make their own decisions, but also that they have the option to complete the minimum amount of work and get a passing grade, or they can exert themselves, put in extra effort, and get a B or an A. The choice is theirs. Teachers who require a minimum amount of work demonstrate trust in their students to choose well, and students who sense that belief and trust tend to live up to and even surpass their teacher's highest expectations for them.

So a few minimum requirements ensure that students make progress toward the course's ultimate objectives while allowing as much individual choice as possible about literature. The kinds of requirements you need to clarify involve the amount of time the student needs to invest; the content, or the literary works to be explored; the process, as in acceptable activities the student may use to explore literary works; and the products, or physical evidence such as essays or reports that document the work that the student has done. Most products serve not only as documentation, but also facilitate learning in some way, such as helping the student to develop skill in understanding and responding to literature.

This chapter will focus primarily on what students read and how they learn; although requirements for responding to literature in writing will be mentioned, the responses to literature that benefit students at the various stages of learning will be discussed in the next chapter.

CONTENT REQUIREMENTS

In terms of content, students need to know what quantity and quality of literature they need to interact with in this course. You might be tempted to just pick an arbitrary number that seems doable and yet challenging and require the student to read that many works, but actually the question of quantity is a little more complicated because the number of books students can tackle in a semester depends on the length and difficulty of the books they're attempting. So before setting any expectation for quantity, think about what quality of reading you want your student to accomplish in this course.

What is the quality you are seeking at this point in your student's development? Younger students who are at the stage where they must develop breadth in their reading projects need that expectation clarified to them with a requirement that demands variety. For instance, they might be required to demonstrate that their choices reflect some minimum number of distinct genres. At the same time, even students whose primary goal is developing breadth should also be gradually building up their skills as readers by sampling a project or two involving greater difficulty as well. Clarify this expectation by requiring students to read a certain number of books that will specifically build up a repertoire of recognizable, serious classic works. As students progress in the program, this expectation for seeing students engage with more books that constitute greater depth will increase, while the expectation for much variety will go down.

Quality Means Classic

For the most part, "quality" in literature refers to literary works that are considered classic. Now, what constitutes classic literature has been debated by philosophers and literary experts, and you should know that there is little agreement as to which books merit classic status. As the term pertains to a work's perceived merit, it is somewhat helpful is to understand the distinction between good and great books. According to Mortimer Adler and Charles Van Doren (1972), good books are those that "convey to the reader significant insights about subjects of enduring interest to human beings" while a very few great or "inexhaustible" books are those that can be turned to time and again without the reader ever exhausting their insights (p. 342, 343).

Most people who talk about classic books are thinking mainly of the first type of book. This, for the most part, is the kind of literature most high school literature courses deal with. Unfortunately, among these good books no canon exists, which is why you will see a lot of variety if you search for lists of classic books on the Internet:

the designation in this regard is entirely subjective. And yet, there is another aspect of what makes literature classic that is entirely objective. This aspect is endurance, and it is a reliable indicator of quality simply because publishers do not issue new printings of books that don't sell. So a book that has stayed in print for a long time must be either very useful or very well-crafted. Especially when you consider that such old books necessarily involve antiquated style and language, something about any book that has remained in print a very long time—say, more than a century—must be exceptionally good. Among good books, that something is generally significant insights.

Books that hold significant insights will naturally stretch the minds of readers. Such books challenge readers to grow and acquire a taste for more challenging books. Quite often, such books work for readers on many levels. On the simplest level, good books are immediately pleasing as entertainment. One can read *Animal Farm* as a simple story that is at times humorous and at times sad. One can also consider the allegory Orwell intended by the story and think about the political statement he made. Finally, one can ponder the deeper implications of the work personally: To what extent am I a Napoleon? Are the ways in which I am a Boxer? The more students experiment with works of enduring quality, the more they will be challenged to interact with these significant insights on multiple levels—both because that is what readers naturally learn to do and because that is what you will gradually teach them through the documented responses you will eventually require.

A book that has endured the test of time will normally be recognized by other readers and, of particular interest for college bound high school students, by the reading community that will consider students' college entrance exams and application essays. In addition, both classic and contemporary authors and other media forms constantly reference classic works. Familiarity with classics enriches all subsequent reading to some degree. For example, not long ago I read a mystery that referred to someone as a "real William Dobbin." Now, coincidentally, I had just read Thackeray's *Vanity Fair*, and so I actually picked up the reference and understood what the author meant by it. Only a few months earlier, I would have probably glossed right over it. I was excited and pleased with my sighting. So not only does familiarity with many classic works lead to greater understanding, from it will spring many small pleasures.

Students should also be encouraged to read classic literature because most recently written fiction can't compare with the quality of most classics. The reason for this should be obvious: only exceptional books endure and become classic, and by definition, a book that is exceptional is the exception to the rule. And the rule is that most books have a short print-life and are just okay: not especially good, not great, and almost never inexhaustible (Adler & Van Doren, p. 343).

But there are other problems with a lot of the more contemporary books being published these days. Many of the contemporary books that are being marketed as young adult fiction are not particularly good in the sense that they lack significant insights about subjects of enduring interest. Some of them try to be significant, but among trendy contemporary fiction books, the meaning all too often is little more than cliché. Most of the popular young adult fiction books out there don't have the potential to instill deeper understanding in a student. All they really do—and in many cases, all they're meant to do—is entertain. That is not meant to disparage such books; after all, sometimes entertainment is precisely what a reader wants and needs.

Another category for contemporary books is 'literary.' These books are the ones that literary people sometimes describe as 'classic' in spite of their relative novelty. Obviously, those people hold a different view of what it means for a literary work to be classic; rather than acknowledging a work's endurance, they appreciate a book for an ideal it upholds or for a particular quality it exudes. Generally, the quality that these literary reviewers appreciate in the books they consider 'classic' will be the way their author captures some purportedly 'authentic' human experience through vivid and seemingly accurate depictions of reality.

There are, however, a couple of problems with contemporary literary fiction. The first is that they tend to be "deep" but cryptic. Often, only English teachers with special training can extract all their hidden meanings, and since they find that activity fulfilling, they think that everyone should be doing likewise. Of course, not everyone agrees with this point of view. Orson Card, whose novella was criticized by literary specialists for its clear, straightforward story, responded in the introduction to his bestselling novella, "If everybody came to agree that stories should be told this clearly, the professors of literature would be out of a job, and the writers of obscure, encoded fiction would be, not honored, but pitied for their impenetrability" (Card, 1991, p. xvi).

The other problem with contemporary literary writing is that it values authenticity over truth. This is significant. Classic authors sought truth through their stories and ponderings, but contemporary postmodern authors reject the notion of universal truth and embrace cultural diversity, which insists that what is right is all a matter of perspective. What postmodern authors attempt to do, therefore, is convince readers of their perspectives by creating authentic pictures of humanity reflecting the injustice they feel is being done to a specific group that the author perceives as oppressed by society. Thus a work of contemporary literary fiction is often a battle cry: "A cultural relativist must care for culture more than truth, and fight for culture while knowing it is not true" (Bloom, 1987, p. 202). This contentious quality strikes readers most forcefully when an author's values opposes their own. Confronted with what they believe to be wrong or false, readers can feel offended and sometimes even violated by works of literary fiction.

That is why I advise homeschooling educators to build a library with genuinely classic works and those contemporary books that appeal to their students without offending their family's values. A library that is rich in truly classic books of significant and decipherable meaning can challenge a student to greater intellectual understanding without being subjected to ideas or images that are shocking, repulsive, weird, or off-putting. Of course, there is no reason you can't include in your library contemporary books that are enjoyable if somewhat less deep than others, but for the most part, the best source for deeper understanding from books is literature that has endured and is truly classic.

Quantity of Quality Books

One of the problems I have had in coming up with a precise number of quality books to recommend for students in general is that the amount of time it takes different students to read varies considerably from student to student, and the amount of time it takes a given student to read a work of literature varies considerably, depending on the work.

The one thing that does not vary by student or work is the amount of time you can reasonably expect students to invest in this course. Every student, whether he or she reads fast or slow, has the same number of hours in a day and the same number of academic courses competing for time. Because the activities of the language arts are so critical to a student's future development and success, it seems reasonable to designate at least two hours for them daily. Of course, that much time represents both literature and composition courses, and I do recommend keeping these courses separate, which means that in the simplest terms, you should expect your student to spend at least one hour reading (or engaging in some other literature-related activity—more on that later) every day.

The next thing to decide is what students should do during that hour, and the answer to this question will come in part from where in the program that student is. If you want your student to have read with breadth and depth by the time he or she finishes high school, you will have to design courses that gradually build the skill in reading and understanding to get there. Thus freshman and sophomore students focus on breadth, exploring a variety of literary works representing different genres, areas of interest, and levels of difficulty. During this time, students build up speed as readers, accumulate knowledge about how books work, and experience a number of recognizably classic books. Each of these initial objectives serves a purpose and enables students to make progress toward reading with greater depth during the junior and senior years.

In order to achieve the objectives of the course, you will need to require students to read works that align with the outcome that is most important at each phase of the program. Early in the program, you want to the student to attempt many reading projects from a set of literary works that you have designated in advance. You want to encourage the student to read a variety of as many good books as possible but also to attempt at least a few projects representing some challenge. The requirements at this stage, then, should ensure that students attain both of these by assigning a minimum quantity of diverse genres the student should attempt, as well as a minimum quantity of classic works which generally represent greater challenge.

For instance, a typical freshman might be required to read literary works from a minimum of six different genres (including at least one non-fiction choice) and a minimum of three modern classics (in print for at least forty years) and two classic works (in print for more than a century) per semester. That may sound overly ambitious for many students, but don't forget that many classic works are not extremely long, and both short story and essays are considered to be literary genres. You might even list one shorter literary work as a requirement, thus enabling students to easily achieve goals and probably enabling them to easily exceed them.

The student would thus be required to read five full-length literary works and one short story in order to earn a C; students who surpass that number in quantity of total works read or who read a higher number of quality selections (that is, the student reads three classics rather than just two) earn either a B or an A. This should be doable for even a relatively slow reader, especially if you offer the student the option of an alternative process for some of those projects.

ALTERNATIVE PROCESSES FACILITATE SUCCESS

If your student reads slowly or struggles with decoding words, I would suggest you offer a few alternative options to your student for completing the classic component of course requirements. According to educational psychologist Diane McGuinness, "in order to understand what you read, you must be accurate and fluent in decoding" (1997, p. 274). Students who struggle with decoding necessarily have a handicap, especially with classic literature that uses a lot of unfamiliar terminology. The need to continually pause to decode impedes fluent reading, which in turn inhibits understanding.

And yet, students who read slowly should not be deprived of the opportunity to experience classic literature. "The answer lies in adjusting [the] program to individual differences by administering it sensitively and flexibly" (Adler, 1982, p. 44). Students who decode slowly must get just as much practice reading as students who decode fluently, but it may be beneficial for these students to build up that fluency by reading books that are more contemporary and entertaining than books that convey challenging ideas through unfamiliar vocabulary. These primarily entertaining books are not totally devoid of literary value: students can use these books to learn the terminology of literature, explore different genres, and discover structural elements in the books they read. At the same time, however, it is important for these students to start building a repertoire of classic works, so that they are not excluded from the community of educated people who hear titles like *Pygmalion* or authors like "Hugo" and still retain their intellectual footing.

How can a student who reads slowly become familiar with many classic literature works? The first and best suggestion I have is to listen to audio versions of unabridged classic works of literature. Since the vocabulary and reading difficulty is usually harder in older works, reading a long classic novel like *One Hundred Years of Solitude* or *War and Peace* really might be unrealistic for slower readers, but there's no reason why even a slow reader can't invest the time in listening to such a novel. Students should have access to a hard copy of the classic works they listen to, however, so that they may follow along as they listen. A hard copy will also be invaluable when the time comes to apply advanced skills like interpreting and analyzing literary works which will require students to locate passages and possibly quote the text appropriately. Websites such as www.librivox.org and www.freeclassicaudiobooks.com make many classic texts available for download for free; also, many public libraries offer audio versions of classic literature through their websites. Just make sure, however, that the version you choose is unabridged.

Struggling readers can also benefit from software such as Universal Reader Plus. This program allows users to highlight any text, and the software program highlights each word as it verbalizes the text. Since this software works not only with word processing documents but with online websites as well, it would be especially valuable for reading any of the many classic texts that are available online through sites such as www.classicreader.com and www.gutenberg.org which make classic books available to readers online for free. Compared with the option of downloading an audio version of a classic text and reading along, using the Universal Reader software allows students to set the pace, so that they can follow along more easily. On the other hand, the narration with software programs is digitally produced; to date, it doesn't narrate texts with the natural intonation and expression of a human voice, and sometimes, it will mispronounce heteronyms (such as 'tear' – that has a long 'e' sound when it means the stuff that comes out of your eyes and a short 'e' when it means to rip paper).

Alternative Activities for Becoming Familiar with Classic Literature

- **Listen to audio versions of unabridged texts and use a hard copy to read along**

- **Use a software program such as Universal Reader to read on-line classics**

- **View a performance of a drama or watch a well-done video adaptation of a classic literary work**

- **Read classics out loud, together**

Another good option is to watch dramas, performed live or on DVD. This is actually a great way for any student to gain familiarity with any dramatic work, because playwrights pen dramas to be performed and viewed, not read. In fact, even students who are fluent readers would benefit from reading dramas only after they've seen them performed. Less fluent readers can benefit from viewing the drama on DVD and then reading or analyzing a specific scene or soliloquy. Somewhat less highly recommended is watching video adaptations of classic novels. This is a little less ideal since converting a novel into a screenplay necessarily alters the literary work—sometimes minimally, but other times significantly or almost beyond recognition. However, that does not mean that video adaptations can't be useful for familiarizing a student with a classic work and providing an appealing preview for the literary work in question. For instance, the writing of Alexandre Dumas has inspired a number of action-packed movies. Watching a movie might convince a wary student that *The Three Musketeers* really might be worth reading.

Still another possibility is to read a classic book out-loud, together. This is an ambitious undertaking, but not only does it familiarize students with great literature, it is a wonderfully bonding family experience. I read both of my daughters *The Lord of the Rings*, and I loved the experience both times. The second time I read it with my younger daughter, she actually had to read the last pages for me as I was sobbing too hard to finish. I always hate saying good-bye to Frodo and Gandalf. And, as Gandalf reminds us, "not all tears are an evil" (p. 310).

Finally, remember that students can fulfill the requirement to read a classic with shorter works like short stories, essays, poems, dramas and novellas. The possibility of ticking off a classic work for reading a mere twenty pages will probably entice your reader to find a few short stories they really like. As a bonus, they'll be pushing themselves to increase the level of challenge they feel comfortable reading, without feeling overwhelmed by a seemingly impossible task. You want your student to be challenged, but not beyond what he or she can reasonably handle.

CONVEYING REQUIREMENTS CLEARLY

How do you make sure your student understands what's expected? You might provide your student a streamlined checklist or offer the student a learning contract. In a sense, it doesn't matter how you convey requirements to your students so long as you are clear about your expectations and any consequences for failing to meet them. It's helpful to put requirements in writing—that way, students have a way of checking back; they also can assess how much of their work they've completed and how much they've got left.

Using a Checklist

The simplest option for clarifying course requirements is a checklist indicating the minimum time students must spend completing course activities as well as whatever quantity and quality of content and products the student must complete. Beyond these guidelines, however, students have complete freedom to read what they want and when, whether to give up on a book they really hate or re-read one they love, read something just for fun, or tackle something hard.

<u>Sample Checklist</u>
Choose books from the designated bookshelf and read for one hour daily. Your selections can include anything on the bookshelf (including re-reading books you have previously enjoyed) so long as you complete the following checklist by the end of the semester:

- ☐ 2 works of classic fiction (written over one hundred years ago) by at least two different authors

- ☐ 2 works of modern classic fiction (written over 40 years ago) by at least two different authors

- ☐ 4 works representing four different fiction genres (realistic contemporary, realistic historical, mystery, suspense, adventure, romance, fantasy, science fiction, drama)

☐ 2 works representing at least two different types of nonfiction (biography, autobiography, memoir, history, humor, instructional, informational)

☐ 2 short works (short story or essay)

☐ A reading log documenting each work read

☐ A written summary of each work read (approximately one paragraph)

Although that list might seem demanding, students maintain control over how much effort they will invest and how much benefit they will derive from their efforts. A student could complete his or her requirements with a minimum of effort, or surpass expectations by putting in a maximum. Compare the way two different students might choose to complete these course requirements:

Jessie might read:

Across Five Aprils by Irene Hunt

Little Women by Louisa May Alcott

O Pioneers by Willa Cather

Emily of New Moon by L.M.M. Montgomery

To Kill a Mockinbird by Harper Lee

Old Yeller by Fred Gipson

Invincible Louisa by Cornelia Meigs

"The Gift of the Magi" by O. Henry

The Princess and the Goblin by George MacDonald

The Princess and Curdie by George MacDonald

"Death of a Pig" (an essay) by E.B. White

The hypothetical Jessie's list is impressive: it includes nine full-length books, plus two shorter works. She easily met and exceeded the requirements, which both allowed her the freedom to indulge her obvious passion for historical fiction but also challenged her to expand her tastes and try a few genres she probably wouldn't have otherwise sought on her own.

Sam might read:

"The Tell-Tale Heart" by Edgar Allen Poe

Fantastic Voyage by Isaac Asimov

XKCD (selected comics)

"Jeeves and the Unbidden Guest" by P.G. Wodehouse

Shane by Jack Schaefer

"Long-Distance Vision" (an essay about aviators Anne Lindbergh and Antoine
de Saint-Exupery) by David McCullough

In contrast to Jessie, Sam doesn't read a lot, but in fact, the list above does complete the checklist requirements. Evidenced here are two classics (Poe and Wodehouse), two modern classics (Asimov and Schaefer), four fiction genres (horror, science fiction, short story, and action), two nonfiction genres (humor and biography), and three short works (two short stories and one essay). In addition, literary works from classic, modern classic, and contemporary periods are included.

What I want you to see, though, is that although Jessie reads significantly more than Sam, both students fulfilled the criteria. This is possible because requirements are both flexible and compatible: the requirement to read works from four different genres, for instance, is compatible with the requirements to read short stories, classics, and modern classics. In addition, some classics are also short stories. Sam, by reading Edgar Allen Poe's "The Tell-Tale Heart" can check off one short story, one genre, and one classic all at once. This kind of flexibility offers students real freedom and yet, as an avid reader like Jessie might find, still challenges students to expand tastes and interests.

Of course, by the time students reach their junior and senior years, objectives will have changed. Students will be reading with greater focus and writing about the books they read. For these students, a more appropriate checklist might look more like this:

<u>Sample Checklist—Senior Year</u>
Choose books from the designated bookshelf and read for one hour daily. Your selections can include anything on the bookshelf (including re-reading books you have previously enjoyed) so long as you complete the following checklist by the end of the semester:

- ☐ Read at least 2 works of classic fiction (written over one hundred years ago).

- ☐ Read at least 2 works of modern classic fiction (written over 40 years ago).

- ☐ Write two literary analyses. You may write about just one of the books you read or you can write about them all. You may want to compare two of the works or contrast two different writing styles, examine the way an author developed a theme or evaluate how well the author achieved a certain effect.

- ☐ Choose a topic and develop a hypothesis about it that you would like to investigate further. Read at least one book and at least three articles about the topic. Write a 7 – 10 page research paper that includes citations from the texts in which you describe your findings.

- ☐ Read at least 9 essays, chapters, or articles about a specific, abstract (i.e., philosophical) concept or idea. Write a 5 – 7 page synthesis paper drawing from those sources and including at least six quotations that clarifies what you believe and why. (Hint: use concrete examples to support your ideas.)

REQUIREMENTS FACILITATE OBJECTIVE GRADING

Along with understanding what is required of them, students need to understand the way they complete requirements translate into a letter grade. Since the course requirements identify the minimum amount of work for passing the course, students must choose to work harder than required in order to earn a better-than-just-passing grade.

According to such a system, a student who completes exactly what is required to complete the course would earn a 'C.' Students who surpass their requirements in some regard earn a 'B', and students who surpass multiple requirements earn an 'A.' On the flip side, students who try but do not quite complete the requirements earn a 'D,' while students who clearly have not attempted and thus not completed the majority of the requirements earn an 'F.'

Grades, therefore, are entirely objective, and students remain absolutely in control of whatever grade they will ultimately get. Also, although I evaluate and provide feedback for written responses, I do not assign grades for written responses at the freshman and sophomore level. I do, however, require them to be done in order to assign the student any grade for completing the course. The philosophy behind this grading system is explained more extensively in the next chapter.

Using a Learning Contract

Another way to ensure that you and your student are on the same page is to use a learning contract. Learning contracts allow students to make choices about the content, process, and products from which they will learn, while allowing teachers to specify their priorities for learning (Tomlinson, 1999, p. 87). The format I like to use for this consists of three columns corresponding to each of these learning variables and three rows with options for each variable. As teacher, your job is to fill in the boxes with options for each aspect of learning that would each satisfy your requirements for passing the course. Once you've filled the table, you offer it to your student so that he or she can select the most appealing options. To visualize what this looks like, see the example on page 56.

The first column in the table lists options for the quantity and quality of content students learn. Try to develop options for reading that involve genuine choice but also real challenge; in addition, try to offer options that will really appeal to your reader. For instance, if your student wants to read nothing but science fiction, offer one option that calls for more variety in authors and periods but perhaps less variety in genres. Your student would still be challenged to explore something new, but hopefully in a way that is still appealing. As with the checklists above, options may allow for overlapping categories: that is, a classic mystery counts as a classic and a genre.

Learning process refers to how students learn this content. In a literature course, reading would normally be the main process for learning content, but teachers of struggling readers might want to identify alternative activities that students may use to complete a certain number of the required reading projects. Of course, any student might benefit from gaining familiarity with literary content through auditory and visual means, which actually facilitates reading especially lengthy or challenging literary works.

Products refer to the written work, documentation or other physical products (perhaps a diorama?) that allow you to evaluate your student's efforts and prove that your student has accomplished the course requirements. These products should document your student's activities and understanding so that you can use them to measure growth when compared with past or future products. Therefore, if you do go with dioramas as an option—and this is not entirely tongue in cheek: some students may derive benefits from some kind of artistic representation of a literary work they read—you might want to add something a little more substantial to this option to make sure you have some way of evaluating progress.

It's important to remember that learning contracts are about individualizing learning, not listing interesting options. Just because an activity facilitates learning for some students does not mean that it will serve yours. Each option in each category should represent the least you will accept of your student for this course. Be careful about offering options that are so accessible that students don't really grow or so appealing they don't really expand their horizons.

The learning contract thus clarifies the course requirements and should function as a binding agreement between you and your student. Whichever options your student selects, make sure you honor that workload; don't add more demands to it later. Also, make sure your student understands how the learning contract works with grading— namely, that the learning contract specifies the least amount of work required for passing the course, and that the student will have to exceed the minimum in order to qualify for an A or B grade.

A worksheet to help you decide what content, processes, and products will best facilitate your student's personal growth and a blank template for a learning contract are available in Appendix D. Here's a sample of a completed learning contract:

Sample Learning Contract

Student __Jessie James__   Semester: __Fall 2011__

Select one option from each column and spend at least one hour daily or five hours weekly engaging in learning the content and completing activities you selected.

Learning Content	Learning Process	Learning Products
Read (or read along to) at least 9 works of history, sociological or historical fiction, biography, or autobiography aligning with our American History course; include at least 4 classics	Read literary works for all required content; in addition to reading, you may watch video adaptations of classic literary works for extra credit	Log and rate each book; mark responses on literary elements worksheets; plus write book reviews for your favorite two literary works
Read (or read along to) at least 9 literary works from at least six distinct genres, including at least three classic and three modern classic works	Read contemporary works and classic short stories; use audio versions or Universal Reader software for full-length classic literary works	Complete a reading log plus written summaries (one paragraph or so) for each literary work you read or view
Read 5 literary works of my choosing and at least 5 literary works of your choosing.	Read three literary works of your choosing; listen to audio versions and read along for the remainder of your required selections	Maintain a reading log via GoodReads.com; also, write a review for three books; participate in at least one on-line book discussion for extra credit

Submit all completed products by ___December 17, 2011___.

(Student and Teacher sign the completed contract.)

Using a Syllabus

Later in the program, objectives shift toward reading with depth. Since this will require more time, students will actually read fewer books overall, but the books they do read will be of greater challenge than before; also, written responses become more significant and take up more of the students' time. Because of this, written responses such as literary analyses, synthesis essays, and research papers merit inclusion in the grading process, although you may want to consider separating the content of papers from the quality of the writing itself. Separating these allows you to assign one grade for the quality of thought stemming from reading, which affects the student's grade in the literature course, and the quality of writing, which affects the student's grade in composition and which, ideally, stems from a clear rubric. (See my book, *Grading with a Purple Crayon*, for more about using rubrics to clarify goals and produce objective grades for high school composition.)

Although students at this stage read with greater focus, the exact nature of this focus may vary. One student may want to spend an entire year exploring American, British, or World literature, exploring a particular genre such as poetry or drama, or examining the works of Shakespeare, mythology, or the Bible. Another possibility is for the student to elect a literature-based approach to another course such as history, geography, philosophy, or science. If at all possible, encourage students to sample the works of at least one or two of the authors that appear on the list of Great Book Authors in Appendix B.

Requirements at this stage, perhaps even more so than before, take on a contractual feel: students commit to a specific focus of their own choosing (with teacher approval, of course) and agree to complete a fairly defined program of difficult reading and written responses. Student choice, at this stage, is less a matter of picking books and more a matter of choosing a focus for the course, some (but perhaps not all) of the reading material, and a general course of action.

Because requirements are necessarily more specific, you may want to consider using a syllabus rather than a checklist or learning contract. According to Grunert O'Brien, Millis and Cohen (2008), a learner-centered syllabus defines student responsibilities and sets the tone for the course (p. 26, 28). A syllabus, apart from identifying expectations and requirements, includes a course schedule which can help students keep track of what is due and when. As before, grading is objective and students retain control of their final grade.

Syllabus components that you might want to include are:

- **Course description:** briefly overviews what the student will learn and how as a result of this course

- **Course objectives:** list the knowledge, skills, and understanding the student should accomplish as a result of the course. A good way to do this is to use a bulleted list of action verbs that complete the statement, "At the end of this course, you should be able to:"

- **Readings:** normally refer to a list of required and optional reading assigned by the instructor and information about where these books may be obtained

- **Resources:** identifies where students can go for extra help or advice

- **Course requirements:** specify exactly what is required in order to pass the course and meet course objectives

- **Course calendar:** provides a dated schedule of any topics to be covered in lectures (probably not applicable for most homeschool situations) and due dates for assignments, projects, and exams

- **Policies and expectations:** spell out what you expect of the student in terms of attitudes, behaviors, participation, and timelines. This would also be an appropriate place to list how, if appropriate, students are to document sources (Chicago, MLA, APA, or other)

- **Evaluation:** informs the student about how you (and your student) will assess progress toward the course objectives

- **Grading procedures:** this item clarifies what work affects the student's grade for the course and shows students how they can control the grade they get

A basic syllabus should provide students with essential information for this course: reading and resource information, course requirements, expectations (especially in terms of the amount of time you expect the student to spend doing work for the course), a course calendar, evaluation and grading procedures.

Sample Syllabus for a Year-Long Literature Course

<u>Course description</u>
In this course, you will view and read several Shakespearean plays. You have the option of choosing from a number of comedies, histories, and tragedies; you will also read essays written by literary experts about the works you choose and write two literary analyses of your own. You will become familiar with several Shakespearean plays, improve your skill in interpretation, and experiment with literary criticism. Your main goal in this course, however, is to find some aspect of Shakespeare's plays—his use of language, character development, weaving of stories, or deeper meaning—that you can appreciate.

<u>Course objectives</u>
After this course, you should be able to:

- Categorize Shakespearean plays as comedy, tragedy, or history
- Describe the basic features and elements of comedy and tragedy
- Recognize characters and basic plots of several plays
- Discuss the meaning of plays based on plots and outcomes
- Analyze some aspect of one or more Shakespearean dramas
- Use evidence from a text to support a point in a literary analysis

<u>Course Readings and Resources</u>
You can peruse options for viewing performances of Shakespearean plays and we'll order them through Netflix. Books for the course can be found on the living room bookcase:

- Copies of 18 plays (*No Fear Shakespeare*)
- Allan Bloom's *Love & Friendship*
- Harold Bloom's *Shakespeare: The Invention of the Human*
- *Northrop Frye on Shakespeare*
- Harold Goddard's *The Meaning of Shakespeare, Volume I*
- Books with background information about the plays
- *Shakespeare A to Z: The Essential Reference*

Course requirements

In order to pass the course with a 'C', you must view, read, and log:

- 3 comedies

- 3 histories

- 3 tragedies

In addition, you must read

- Background information about Shakespeare

- 5 literary analysis essays about plays you choose

Finally, you will need to write:

- One literary analysis exploring one or comparing two or more plays

- One literary analysis examining a theme that occurs in two or more plays

Course calendar

Most of the dates on this calendar are flexible and serve mainly to help you stay on track; however, written products are due no later than the date listed (so I can turn your grades in to our advisor).

Assignment	Due Date
Read background information	August 26
Begin comedies unit	August 29
Finish comedies unit	December 2
Topic/thesis for literary analysis—see me for approval	December 2
Begin histories unit	December 5
Minimum 4 plays read and viewed by mid-point	December 15
Literary Analysis 1 and Semester I Reading/Viewing Log	January 6
Finish histories unit	February 24
Begin tragedies unit	February 27
Topic/thesis for literary analysis—see me for approval	April 13
Finish tragedies unit	May 11
Literary Analysis 2, Final Reading/Viewing Log Due	May 14

Policies and expectations

You will be expected to spend at least five hours weekly reading, viewing, discussing, or responding to Shakespeare's plays. You will need to take responsibility for finding DVDs for the plays that interest you; please arrange with me a time to view DVD performances together. See me before you begin your literary analysis and I will either approve your thesis or help you refine your topic. I expect you to come to me if you get stuck or have questions about writing a literary analysis.

Evaluation and Grading

Your grade for this course will reflect the thoroughness of your work toward completing the course requirements as documented on your reading/viewing log and the quality of your literary analyses. The reading and viewing aspect of the course is worth 67% of your grade. If you complete exactly the requirements of the course, you will receive a 'C.' If you read or view more plays than are required, your grade will reflect your efforts. The writing aspect of the course is worth 33% of your grade and will be calculated using the rubric below.

Grading for the Reading and Viewing Aspect of the Course

A = you surpass the course requirements significantly by viewing and reading more plays or reading more essays than required (three or more additional plays/essays)

B = you surpass requirements slightly by reading or viewing one or two plays or essays more than required

C= you meet the course requirements

D = you read and view one or two fewer plays or literary essays than required

F = you read and view three fewer plays than required

Grading for the Writing Aspect of the Course

Criteria	1 point	2 points	3 points
Purpose	The writer summarizes the work or attempts to interpret or evaluate it in a reflective manner	The writer attempts to make sense of a character or a plot or compares similar literary works	The writer attempts to interpret meaning, examine some purpose or technique of the author, or evaluate the effect of a literary work
Content:	The thesis does not identify the author or title of the literary work or makes no assertion about the text	The thesis statement refers to a literary work but what it asserts is unclear	The thesis statement names the author and literary work(s) and makes a clear assertion about the work(s)
Authoritative Support	The writer fails to support assertions with evidence from the text	The writer supports assertions with evidence from the text; however, the writer relies too heavily on extensive quotations	The writer supports assertions with evidence from the text, preferring summary and paraphrase and integrating quotations judiciously and smoothly
Citations	The writer fails to include source information or page numbers for quoted material or includes no references or works cited page	The writer includes source information and a page number for quoted material; however, errors exist in the formatting of entries on the bibliography	The writer includes source information and a page number for all quoted material in the composition; formatting and entries on the bibliography are correct

So requirements really do allow students a great deal of freedom: the checklist, learning contract, or syllabus tells students what they need to accomplish, but students decide what they want to read, how and how well they want to complete the various requirements, and whether they want to meet them or surpass them. Requirements allow you as teacher to guarantee forward movement; minimizing those requirements allows students to retain the control they need to feel respected and empowered.

CHAPTER V
RESPONDING RESPECTFULLY

Make learning an almost errorless process.
—Patricia Logan Oelwein

THE CHALLENGE:

How can a teacher be sure a student is learning? When a parent is a teacher, how can evaluation remain objective? To what degree can students control the grades they receive?

How would you feel if you ran into a friend and, upon learning that you had both read a certain book, the friend began to ask trivial questions about the contents of the book, as if to see how well you had read it? I don't know about you, but I'd feel irritated. But what if this person seemed to be purposefully asking pointless questions just to trip you up? How would you feel then? Personally, I'd feel disrespected.

Of course, no reasonable person would ever do such a thing. In real life and among reasonable people, friends ask one another how well they liked books they've both read, and friends answer with more or less detail, depending on whether they liked the book or not and whether their friend seems to agree with their assessment. In real life, people don't use books to test one another, they use them to strengthen bonds and encourage one another in the love of true and beautiful things.

Respecting your student as a real reader is one of the most important things you can do to encourage the propensity to love reading wisely and well, but at the same time, as a teacher, you do have an obligation to make sure your student is profiting. How do you know your student has benefited from reading? Liking books is not the same as being stretched by them. How do you know growth has occurred?

To a certain extent, it will be possible to discern growth just by observing how your student's choices and attitudes have changed over time. But as a conscientious educator, it's important also to measure progress. Tyler (1949) recommends "at least two appraisals—one taking place in the early part of the educational program and the other at some later point so that the change may be measured" (p. 106). He goes on to recommend annual appraisals: Students tend to forget a good deal of the material that they learn for tests, making it necessary to evaluate not only learning but also its permanence (p. 107).

Two implications seem obvious: first, tests that require students to recall literature-related information—say about figurative devices or trivia about a certain author or book—serve almost no purpose: they can't show growth, except to show that a student knows something he or she did not know before, and they don't imply permanence, in that students are likely to forget such information anyway. Secondly, more valuable than a series of unrelated tests and essays whose scores you average to arrive at a grade is a portfolio kept over the course of four years containing the student's reading logs and written responses to literature. These documents provide multiple appraisals and clearly show expanding tastes, interests, and purposes for reading as well as increasingly sophisticated insights and skill in understanding.

And notice that these are the course objectives you want to measure. Reading logs track the student's growth in the breadth—or diversity of tastes and interests—and depth—or level of challenging vocabulary, structure, themes and concepts—your student has perused and gained skill in reading over time.

For instance, you can see the progress in both breadth and depth just by comparing the kinds of books Kristen was reading as a freshman versus what she read as a senior: whereas as a freshman, she chose to read only nonfiction books about her favorite topics—books like *Born Free*—as a senior, she was exploring new areas of interest such as social trends and nutrition. As a freshman, Kristen chose fiction primarily for its value for entertainment (even Orwell and Twain were not really as appealing to her for their deeper meaning); as a senior, Kristen was comparing the effectiveness of writing strategies adopted by authors like Austen and Gaskell and evaluating the arguments of Hamilton, Madison and Jay against those of Patrick Henry, George Mason, and Thomas Jefferson. It's easy to see that growth occurred.

Books Kristen Read During High School, Fall Semester

Freshman	Sophomore	Junior	Senior
Watership Down by Richard Adams	*Foundation and Earth* by Isaac Asimov	*A Midsummer's Night's Dream* by William Shakespeare	*The Tipping Point* by Malcolm Gladwell
Born Free by Joy Adamson	*2001: A Space Odyssey* by Arthur Clarke	*Wormholes: The Cosmic Search for Interstellar Shortcuts* by Paul Halpern	*The Federalist* by Alexander Hamilton, John Jay and James Madison
Animal Farm by George Orwell	*I Heard the Owl Call my Name* by Margaret Craven	*Twelfth Night* by William Shakespeare	*What the Anti-Federalists Were For* by Herbert Storing
The Princess Bride by William Goldman	*The Man who was Thursday* by G.K. Chesterton	*The Merchant of Venice* by William Shakespeare	*The Anti-Federalist Papers* edited by Ralph Ketcham
"A Dog's Life" by Mark Twain	*Mythology* by Edith Hamilton	*A Brief History of Time* by Stephen Hawking	*North and South* by Elizabeth Gaskell
A Connecticut Yankee in King Arthur's Court by Mark Twain	*Sense and Sensibility* by Jane Austen	*Romeo and Juliet* by William Shakespeare	*The China Study* by T. Colin Campbell and Thomas M. Campbell II
The Time Machine by H.G. Wells	*The Old Man and the Sea* by Ernest Hemingway	*The Taming of the Shrew* by William Shakespeare	
Never Cry Wolf by Farley Mowat	*A Little Princess* by Frances Burnett		
The Chocolate War by Robert Cormier			
"A Report to the Academy" by Franz Kafka			

So having your student maintain a reading log over the course of four years allows you to document growth in the breadth and depth of his or her reading selections. Appendix E provides a sample template for a reading log that you can copy for your student's use.

A log of the student's reading selections will provide documentation of breadth and depth in regard to the student's tastes and interests, but it can't provide evidence of growth in terms of understanding. An immature student can decode *Romeo and Juliet* and grasp the basic plot, but a student who has truly benefited from a literature course will also engage with it and truly understand (or care) what Shakespeare was saying in it and how he achieved certain effects with it. What was Mercutio's Queen Mab speech all about? Students who haven't developed a propensity to read with depth rarely care about such questions—or rather, they generally care only if their grades depend on it, and even then, they tend only to understand what their teacher has told them. Students who have developed skill in reading with greater depth, however, inevitably find something in the good and great books they read that they want to explore more closely.

I am convinced that this propensity, like that of appreciating literature, develops more or less naturally over time, and the most appropriate role for a teacher is almost that of a midwife that skillfully offers assistance and encouragement, but ultimately must allow the student to do the real work. When teachers try to take it over, rarely do students develop the ability to interpret meaning, nor do they develop the propensity to want to. Giving students too much information about how a work has been interpreted by others or what in it impresses experts discourages students and convinces them that making meaning of literature is the stuff of schoolwork, not the stuff of real life.

Vine and Faust (1993) point out that "assigning books and book reports as the major way to promote a love of reading; providing background information, lists of vocabulary words, purposes for reading, and follow-up questions . . . using tests and theme papers as the major way to evaluate students' reading abilities" actually "disempower readers' abilities to make meaning" of the books they read (p. 93). In each of these activities, the teacher controls the ideas that students are expected to ponder, not the students; from such activities, students learn to respond to the teacher's or the curriculum's concerns, but not to interpret meaning personally. Tyler (1949) notes that "it should, of course, be obvious that the student learns to think through the experience of solving problems for himself. He has not acquired the objective when the teacher does the problem solving and the student only watches" (p. 70). Unless students choose and make sense of books for themselves, the exercise becomes personally meaningless— and who would ever willingly choose to engage in meaningless activity?

So why are nearly all of those practices practically standard in English classes? Oelwein (1995) suggests that many teachers and curriculums do not understand the difference between teaching and testing. Teaching implies imparting knowledge and helping students to learn, while testing serves mainly to help teachers gather evidence about what students know. Unfortunately, many curriculums designed to teach students to understand literature actually just test them on what they know. Oelwein (1995) cites a study in which a group of teachers estimated spending 20% of their class time teaching reading comprehension. But, "when researchers went into the classroom and measured how much of the reading time these teachers actually spent on teaching comprehension, they discovered that the teachers were spending 20 percent of the reading time testing comprehension" (p. 57).

Quizzes and tests do not teach students anything; rather, they serve the educator's need to gather evidence and document learning. Unfortunately, such activities do not actually show growth in a student's level of understanding—for the most part, they only measure a student's ability to recall information. That is not the same as the ability to engage with a work of literature and be challenged by it personally, to desire to explore the questions it poses further, and to evaluate its effectiveness—not because a student has to, but because a student wants to.

MEASURING UNDERSTANDING

One of the best parts of being a homeschooling parent is that I can eliminate testing and focus on teaching and coaching my students early in their high school program, and eventually moving on to what Adler (1982) calls "the Socratic mode of teaching," which involves stimulating students by asking questions, "helping students to raise their minds up from a state of understanding or appreciating less to a state of understanding or appreciating more" (p. 29).

Following Adler's *Paideia Proposal*, this aspect of the literature program involves three stages: first, the student acquires useful knowledge about literature; second, the student develops skill in interpreting literature; and finally, the student applies both knowledge and skill through discussions (both written and verbal) that enlarge understanding. These stages coincide neatly with the reading students typically read at each stage of the program. Initially, most students will gravitate toward books that serve simpler purposes, such as to amuse or inform. Such books may lack powerful themes, but their plots are generally fairly easy to discover. As students move on, they develop more skill in interpreting books and begin to apply the knowledge they've acquired, making connections about what the author is doing and why. Often, students discover deeper meaning by re-reading the same books they read and enjoyed read earlier, deriving more from the same books by glossing over the obvious during the second reading and attending to what was missed during the first reading. This is a good reason to permit students to re-read books if they choose and even to suggest that students postpone writing about a book until they have read it twice. Finally, as students accumulate experience, they tend to choose more complicated literature. They might read George Eliot's *Middlemarch*, which examines sociological and psychological developments through multiple plot-lines, and actually want to pick apart the structural elements or compare the characters against one another to see what Eliot was trying to convey. This is something a student who has acquired knowledge and developed skill in interpreting literature may relish if *Middlemarch* is the type of book that student would normally choose to read.

Measuring growth in understanding, as with breadth and depth, can be achieved by comparing the type of work your student is capable of completing from year to year. In this case, however, rather than comparing reading selections, you compare products: the written work your student completes in response to reading. The type of activity students capably engage in documents growth in understanding: freshman classify, junior analyze; sophomores answer proposed questions, seniors propose and answer their own. By the time students complete the four year literature program, they have gone from learning literary elements and writing concise summaries to engaging with literature, critiquing it, and culling from it great insights.

How do I know my student has grown in her ability to understand? All I have to do is pull out my portfolio of her work. When Kristen was a freshman, she summarized the books she read. When she was a sophomore, she began writing five-paragraph essays about them in answer to the prompts I gave her. As a junior, she started analyzing Shakespeare, exploring questions she had and positing answers, finding evidence in the text. Senior year, she was evaluating the effectiveness of authors' arguments and stories. The products Kristen could produce as a senior versus what she was capable of as a freshman demonstrate growth in understanding.

Stages in the Literary Program

	FIRST STAGE	SECOND STAGE	THIRD STAGE
TIMEFRAME	Freshman – Sophomore	Sophomore – Junior	Junior – Senior Year
MAIN OUTCOME	Knowledge about how literature works; knowledge about specific literary works	Skill in interpreting; skill in exploring ideas in writing	Understanding oneself and the world better
PRIMARY ACTIVITIES	Reading and classifying many literary works	Reading and responding to questions that require students to apply knowledge to specific literary works	Reading the thoughtful writing of others, engaging in thoughtful discussions, and exploring interesting ideas about one or more literary works
PRODUCTS THAT PROVIDE PRACTICE AND DOCUMENT PROGRESS	Reading log, classification checklists, book summaries	Summaries, book reviews, short answers to guided questions (oral or written response)	Deductive or inductive literary analysis or reflection
TEACHER'S ROLE	Acquire literature; direct student to resource materials such as background information; oversee checklists and reading logs	Ask questions or use worksheets to prompt students toward deeper insights about literature (complete orally or in writing); challenge students to devise summaries or to produce thoughtful reviews	Read the same books as your student (or find a community of readers where the student can engage in meaningful discussions); discuss aspects of the work that worked or didn't work, that seemed to hold meaning, or that explored an interesting idea; respond to students' interpretations and evaluations with respect

First Stage: Learning Elements, Gathering Knowledge

Understanding any work of literature requires the student to "grasp the unity of the whole work" and to understand that "the unity of a story is always in its plot" (Adler & Van Doren, 1972, p. 209). The first stage for students who are developing skill in understanding literature, therefore, is that of discovering the structural elements involved in works of fiction that make up that unity. These elements are relatively easy to pick out especially in genre fiction, such as mysteries, thrillers, romances, and action stories which provide wonderful fodder for students who are picking up speed as readers, sampling diverse genres, and reading more or less for fun: in such stories, the climax is always obvious, and the main characters always want the same sorts of nice, obvious things like to survive in a thriller or to find out who did it in a mystery, to find true love in a romance or to avenge a wrong in an action story. By reading lots and lots of relatively simple plots, students gain familiarity with terms and a basic understanding of how authors use plots to unify a story.

As I have reiterated, the focus of the literature program during this first stage is on students reading and experimenting with as many types of literary works as possible; the less you interfere with students' reading, the better. That means that any assignments stemming from reading should take as little time and require as little effort of students as possible. Specifically, it is a bad idea to assign book reports or essays of any kind about the books students read: such assignments make reading feel like work and discourage students from reading many books quickly. The exception, of course, is the student who wishes to write about a particular book—never discourage a student who is motivated to explore any topic in writing.

I have developed a set of checklists that require just a few minutes to complete but instruct students about the structural elements in literature. These worksheets (found in Appendix F) provide students practice in applying general knowledge about how stories work and simultaneously reinforce that knowledge by defining terms. Students learn by doing. As a bonus, the checklists can serve as another form of documentation which demonstrates evidence of learning.

Second Stage: Answering Open-Ended Questions about Texts

When students know the structural elements involved in literature, they will be ready to practice using what they know about the setting, plot, and characters to derive deeper meaning from the work. Now aware of how these elements work, students apply this knowledge to specific works of literature in order to come up with an interpretation by themselves. To facilitate this, I have developed a set of worksheets (found in

Appendix G) to help students clarify for themselves how authors embed meaning in different types of writing. Once again, skill develops through practice, so at this point in the program, students should still be spending more time reading than writing about the books they read.

That being said, students benefit from beginning to practice summarizing the books they read. This need not be terribly demanding, nor indeed should summaries be particularly long. Succinct summaries (as few as four or five sentences long) afford students practice in incorporating all of the essential elements of a novel, reinforce the importance of the structural elements, and provide excellent practice for students learning to write concisely, a skill that will be useful in nearly every piece of academic writing a student will ever encounter. Samples and lessons for students unfamiliar with writing a summary can be found in Appendix H.

Third Stage: Understanding the Meaning of Difficult Texts

So far, the emphasis in the literature program is on building skills through practicing reading many books. During the junior and senior years, the emphasis turns to reading more challenging books. By this time, the student will have achieved the level of understanding necessary to appreciate a truly challenging work of fiction like *Great Expectations, The Brothers Karamazov,* or *Les Miserables.* Naturally, such books take students much longer to read than the simpler works sampled earlier.

Third and fourth year literature students are ready to apply their newly developed skills in reading fiction to more difficult and usually classic texts. Satisfaction, they have found, comes from finding meaning in great books, and at this level, students are able to critically analyze whether or not a novel "worked." In a sense, they have arrived as readers: they have matured to a level of sophistication at which their evaluation holds weight—and when students get to this point, they know it. It is a wonderful feeling to feel confident in one's ability to read and understand difficult literature.

Up until now, students read voluminously and did not delve deeply into meaning. Now, students read with focus and think deeply about meaning. If there is any way you possibly can, try to read the few challenging works your student chooses to examine either in advance or at the same time so that you can interact about the works together. Discussing a great work of literature is one of life's great pleasures. Yes, I understand that this means extra work for you as a teacher, and yes, I understand that as a parent-teacher you have other obligations and maybe teach younger students as well. Nevertheless, I cannot emphasize enough the value of a teacher both facilitating and modeling serious engagement with the ideas contained in great literary works.

Discussing great books instills in readers a desire to explore deeper, and this deeper exploration takes the form of writing about texts. No longer is the goal to read widely and gain practice as before; now students benefit from deliberating over each project. Such careful deliberation merits preservation, and students sense that taking the time to craft a literary analysis is worthwhile. Therefore, documentation for this stage of the literature program takes the form of literary analyses, in which students explore a particular aspect of a particular literary work or compare two or more works, supporting their ideas with evidence from the text.

What students explore in writing should come from the questions or passionate concerns that students themselves feel about a text. In fact, writing about what a teacher or curriculum identifies as important in a work actually shortchanges the student of the opportunity to develop their own powers: "Students are never told what to think before they have a chance to develop their own powers of observation, deduction, and evaluation" (Andrews & Andrews, 2004, p. 12). Examples of two literary analyses that I wrote—one to solidify an idea that was important to me, and one to clarify my thoughts and evaluate the effectiveness of a work—and a list of the types of questions students might wish to explore can be found in Appendix I.

GRADING PHILOSOPHY FOR THE COURSE

The object in this chapter has been to discuss the importance of seeing progress and growth in students. Obviously, it is important to you to know that your student is learning and growing, and as a homeschooling parent, you know that of all people, you are probably the least objective evaluator. This chapter shows you how you can objectively show growth and progress by documenting how your student is understanding at each stage of growth: your initial documentation shows a student capable only of recognizing structural elements in books, subsequent documentation reflects increasing ability to use structural elements to find meaningful connections, and ultimately, your documentation will consist of critical literary analyses that demonstrate a sophisticated level of understanding. Growth is apparent and objective: the student demonstrates a capability to relate to literature in a completely different manner at the end of the program as at the beginning.

But while this evaluation of growth is important for educators, I would not put a grade on this demonstration of understanding. I agree with Tomlinson that assessments should be more about "helping students grow than with cataloging their mistakes" (1999, p. 11).

Here's why. Good grades feel like rewards to students, who know that students who do well get A's. Students who try hard but don't get A's feel discouraged and gradually lose their enthusiasm for learning. Especially in the area of literature, where the outcome you want to see in students is the propensity to read with breadth and depth for the purposes of personal growth and pleasure, it does not make any sense to punish the student if he or she simply does not understand at the level he or she someday will, given the patient nurturing and consistent coaching this type of understanding requires.

A heading in a book I have about Down syndrome reads: "Make learning an almost errorless process" (Oelwein, p. 52). The book isn't aimed at high school literature students, but I love the concept and find it applicable. Why reward some students for grasping concepts rapidly, if that is their natural pace? Why punish others for learning a little more slowly? When it comes to understanding, students always want to do their best. Students may not always want to comply, but no one wants to not understand. Therefore, rather than rewarding how quickly a student learns to understand literature, I would encourage you to reward the effort students put into interacting with it, regardless of the stage of understanding they're operating at.

This takes us back to the checklists and learning contracts discussed earlier in the previous chapter as a means of making course requirements clear to students. Determine what activities your student needs to complete to meet the minimum requirement for your literature course, and make sure those requirements are clear to your student. By incorporating both reading and writing activities into that checklist, you can simultaneously document your student's growth and use that documentation to evaluate whether or not the instruction you have provided has been effective. And if your student isn't learning or growing from these activities, it's up to you to figure out what needs to change in order for those things to happen.

Make sure your student understands that his or her grade for this course depends upon how well activities are completed. Traditionally, an A did not mean that a student had satisfactorily completed requirements but rather that a student had actually excelled and surpassed them. A's, once upon a time, were hard to get.

Such a grading philosophy has its merits and its drawbacks. On the plus side, students are rewarded for working hard and excelling. On the downside, students who meet the course requirements get a 'C' on their transcript. That's a bit of a disadvantage because most teachers these days give a 'C' only to indicate mediocre or even poor work, and colleges consider transcripts seriously. You really don't want a 'C' on a transcript if your student is doing reasonably well.

However, there is no reason your student shouldn't achieve an 'A' in this course. In fact, this is one reason I encourage you to require the least of students, not the most. Students normally want to surpass the expectations set of them as long as the expectations are reasonably doable. So set the bar low—not so low that they're insulted, but low enough that they have the freedom to choose a challenging project that takes them longer to read or to take on more projects than you require.

Grading, then, looks something like this:

A = the student surpasses expectations significantly by reading and responding to the equivalent of two books in addition to the number of books required or by reading two books representing greater challenge, or any combination of these

B = the student surpasses expectations slightly by reading and responding to one book in addition to the number of books required or by fulfilling requirements with at least one book reflecting significant challenge

C = the student reads and responds to the required quantity and quality of books

D = the student reads and responds to fewer than the required quantity of books required but does complete some of the required work

F = the student fails to read and respond as required

For the most part, I recommend you require documentation but not grade it; treat it as pass/fail, or simply explain to your student that his or her work is not done until documentation has been completed. If you suspect your student is not taking the documentation process seriously because you don't grade it or if your student appears not to be learning, you may have to adjust your strategy. Try going over the student's work together and discussing the student's responses. If the student understands but is doing shoddy work, he or she will probably change tactics to avoid the redundant effort of having to talk about it with you, but if the student truly doesn't understand, you can address any misconceptions as they become apparent.

A potential exception to the pass/fail suggestion involves significant responses such as a literary analysis essay. The amount of effort a student invests in such a document deserves a carefully considered assessment on your part. However, I would suggest that any grade you assign this effort on your student's part should reflect your student's ability to meet the specific objectives set out in a clear rubric such as the one on page 62. For more information about designing and using rubrics, see my companion book, *Grading with a Purple Crayon: A Developmental Approach to High School Composition for Homeschooling Families*.

RESPONDING TO YOUR READER

One of the best things you can do to enhance your student's experiences with literature is to be willing and available to respond to your reader as a sounding board and a cheerleader, a fellow enthusiast and a critic. Here are a few suggestions for keeping your responses encouraging and respectful:

Be interested! Ask questions about what your student is reading and how it rates so far. If it sounds interesting, back off and let the book do its own work. But if a book isn't working for your student, do a little probing. Is the book moving too slowly? Are the characters disagreeable? Does it lack the least sense of humor? Is it time to give up and move on to something more appealing?

Be reasonable! If you don't want to know the answer to a question, don't ask it! That means, if you have read *Pride and Prejudice* and you know what the name of Darby's estate is, don't quiz your student on that knowledge. Obviously, ask questions if you want to know what the student has to say in response. For instance, if you genuinely want to know what a book is about and whether it's any good so that you can decide if you want to read it or not (that is, after all, why reasonable people ask such questions), then by all means pick your student's brain.

Be committed! Setting up this student-driven literature course, a huge commitment in and of itself, is not enough. Get busy finding books in your library to read yourself. Discover what you like and don't like. Re-read books you enjoyed in the past—are they still as good as you remembered? Try new authors and genres and challenge yourself to read classics you always meant to read but never got around to. Then tell your student what books you're reading and how you like them. Recommend the best ones—but don't assign them. And if your student recommends a book to you, give it a try!

Be authentic! Don't think you don't have the time to join your student on this journey. You do. You have 24 hours every day, just like the rest of us, and if you're serious about homeschooling a high school student, you will have to model the behaviors you want to see him or her develop. Teenagers value authenticity, so be honest with them. If you've never liked a classic in your life, admit it. Then get to work, figuring out how both of you can learn to appreciate a few classics. You might want to sample a few well-done DVDs to help you get motivated. You might be surprised to find that you like them better when you have the freedom to pick the ones that appeal to you. I've listed a few of our favorites in Appendix B.

Be opinionated! Discuss, discern, disagree—but be don't insist that you're right just because you're the adult or because you read it in college and you still remember what your professor said in his lecture. Instead, treat your reader as a maturing interpreter of literature and demand reasons for his or her intriguing positions. Ask what evidence in the book provides support for the point your student is making, and if you disagree, be ready to pull out some support for your own. And, at the end of the day, if you both still disagree, agree that it is an interesting point and leave it there. It does not matter so much who is right but that your student learn what it is to really care about a book and want to defend his or her own experience of it. That's exciting stuff!

CONCLUSION

In this book, I've argued that you can do better for your high school student than anyone else, and I've given you a number of reasons why and a number of ideas for how this can be so. Here's the high school literature course I'm suggesting in a nutshell:

Focus on a single, clear outcome:

> the student's propensity to read with breadth and depth

Allow your student as much freedom as possible

> to choose what to read and when

Entice your student with accessible and appealing literary works

> that provide challenge and help him or her grow

Clarify a few minimum requirements

> to steer your student in the right direction

Evaluate your student

> by comparing the student's products from year to year

Encourage your student

> by responding with respect, enthusiasm and fellowship

This literature program represents a journey that students will hopefully continue throughout life. Your part in this program is not pointing your student in the right direction but joining him or her by either beginning or continuing a journey of your own. Hopefully, you will both find many friends along this journey, but curiously, your journeys are never quite the same. Your unique tastes and interests will gradually reveal that this journey is very personal; it involves maturing and growing in wisdom. That is the beauty of literature. Wonderfully universal, generously inviting, good literature calls out to seekers of all things lovely and bids them come, join the great community of readers who have begun the reader's odyssey.

References

Adler, M. (1982). The Paideia proposal: An educational manifesto. New York: Simon and Schuster.

Adler, M. & Van Doren, C. (1972). How to read a book: The classic guide to intelligent reading. New York: Simon & Schuster.

Alaska content standards for English/Language arts. (1995). State of Alaska Department of Education & Early Development. Retrieved May 17, 2010 from http://www.eed.state.ak.us/contentStandards/

Andrews, A. & Andrews, M. (2004). Teaching the classics: A Socratic method for literary education. WA: The Center for Literary Education.

Atwell, N. (1998). In the middle: New understandings about writing, reading, and learning. Portsmouth, NH: Boynton/Cook.

Bain, K. (2004). What the best college teachers do. USA: Harvard University Press.

Bloom, A. (1987). The closing of the American mind. New York: Simon & Schuster.

Bloom, A. (1993). Love & friendship. New York: Simon & Schuster.

Card, O. (1991). Ender's game. New York: Tom Doherty Associates, LLC.

Dewey, J. (1938). Experience and education. New York: Simon & Schuster.

Frye, N. (1986). Northrup Frye on Shakespeare. USA: Yale University Press.

Gaskell, E. (1995). North and south. New York: Penguin.

Glasser, W. (1988). Choice theory in the classroom. New York: HarperCollins.

Grandin, T. & Johnson, C. (2005). Animals in translation: Using the mysteries of autism to decode animal behavior. USA: Simon & Schuster.

Grunert O'Brien, J., Millis, B., & Cohen, M. (2008) The course syllabus: A learning-centered approach. USA: Jossey-Bass.

Haddon, M. (2003). The curious incident of the dog in the night-time. USA: Random House.

Hauerwas, S. (2000). A better hope: Resources for a church confronting capitalism, democracy, and postmodernity. Grand Rapids, MI: Brazos Press.

Kirby, G., Goodpaster, J., & Levin, M. (2001). Critical thinking. Boston, MA: Pearson Custom Publishing.

L'Engle, Madeleine. (2001). Madeleine L'Engle herself: Reflections on a writing life. Colorado Springs, CO: WaterBrook Press.

McGuinness, D. (1997). Why our children can't read and what we can do about it: A scientific revolution in reading. New York: Simon & Schuster.

Montessori, M. (1967). The absorbent mind. New York: Dell.

National Council of Teachers of English & International Reading Association. (n.d.). The standards for the English language arts. Retrieved 10/2/11 from http://www.ncte.org/standards

Oelwein, P. (1995). Teaching reading to children with Down syndrome: A guide for parents and teachers. Bethesda, MD: Woodbine House.

Siegel, B. (1996). The world of the autistic child: Understanding and treating autistic spectrum disorders. USA: Oxford University Press.

Tolkien, J. (1955). The return of the king. New York: Quality Paperback Book Club.

Tomlinson, C. (1999). The differentiated classroom: Responding to the needs of all learners. Alexandria, VA: Association for Supervision and Curriculum Development

Treffert, D. (2010). The autistic savant. Wisconsin Medical Society. Retrieved June 14, 2010 from http://www.wisconsinmedicalsociety.org/savant_syndrome/savant_articles/autistic_savant

Truby, J. (2007). The anatomy of a story: 22 steps to becoming a master storyteller. USA: Faber and Faber.

Tyler, R. (1949). Basic principles of curriculum and instruction. Chicago, IL: The University of Chicago Press.

Vine, H. & Faust, M. (1993). Situating readers: Students making meaning of literature. Urbana, IL: National Council of Teachers of English.

Wiggins, G. & McTighe, J. (2005). Understanding by design. Upper Saddle River, NJ: Pearson Education.

STUDENT TASTES AND INTERESTS

Instructions: In the oval labeled 'Taste in Literary Genres,' list the types of books that you have most enjoyed reading in the past. Try to identify at least five. In the oval labeled 'Interests,' list anything you find interesting. If you have a hard time getting started, consult the lists below for a few ideas to get you started.

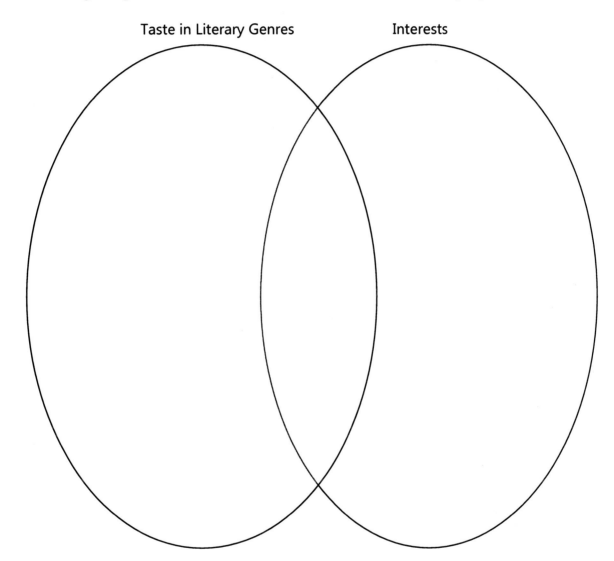

Taste in Literary Genres   Interests

Genres: Science Fiction, Humor, Drama, Fantasy, Historical Fiction, Expository, Thriller, Informative, Poetry, Adventure, How-to, Mystery, Romance, Realistic Fiction, Action, Suspense, Biography, History, Western, Autobiography, Memoir, Coming-of-Age, Psychological, Adventure, Parable, Short Story

Potential Interests: Animals, Sports, Nature, Science, Astronomy, Outdoor Adventures, Dance, Music, Drama, Friends, Reading, Writing, Math, History, Food, Movies, Cars, Trucks, Military, Technology, Construction, Engineering, Children, Politics, Religion, Travel, Foreign Languages

BOOK RECOMMENDATIONS

These lists suggest good options for books to read from a number of genres that are appropriate for high school students. Most of the books I recommend can be understood and have themes that are unambiguous, the only exceptions being nonfiction books (which have theses, not themes) and a few of the more episodic titles, some of which involve many little philosophical lessons, such as *Winnie-the-Pooh* or *The Little Prince*.

My brief descriptions are not meant to summarize the stories in any way—I leave that to students—but only to help you get a sense for how each title is distinct and whether it might appeal to your reader. As you will probably observe, my tastes affect the enthusiasm with which I describe books; in fact, some of the titles here serve mainly to provide variety for readers whose tastes are not my own. Of course, my literary tastes will differ from yours and those of your students, but I offer these suggestions with the hope that they will prove useful to you as you collect good and great literature for your student.

Mystery

A mystery involves discovering the truth about someone or something. Dorothy Sayers suggested that mystery was the natural successor of the action stories that were so popular right up until the end of the age of exploration: "If one could no longer hunt the manticore, one could still hunt the murderer; if the armed escort had grown less necessary, yet one still needed the analyst to frustrate the wiles of the poisoner" (as cited in Hauerwas, p. 205). In a sense, that is what a mystery is: a great hunt to find out the truth. Most mysteries share some variation on that theme. There are so many great mystery writers out there, but Agatha Christie and Doyle's Sherlock Holmes stories are probably the best entry point to the genre.

The Hound of the Baskervilles by Sir Arthur Conan Doyle
The only Sherlock Holmes novel; most of Doyle's stories are short. Students who wanted to sample a short mystery should look for one of many compilations of Sherlock Holmes stories.

Murder on the Orient Express by Agatha Christie
Widely considered the greatest mystery writer ever, Christie really does manage to surprise her readers every time. Happily, there are dozens of Agatha Christie mysteries for those who like her style.

Strong Poison by Dorothy Sayers
Sayers' Lord Peter Wimsey is an untraditional sleuth; somewhat like Agatha Christie's books, Sayers keeps her readers guessing until the end.

Teatime for the Traditionally Built by Alexander McCall Smith
Set in Gabarone, Bostwana, Smith's series weaves several mysteries together. These books aren't terribly fast-paced, but they are, somehow, friendly.

Puddin'head Wilson by Mark Twain
The first mystery in which fingerprinting appears.

A Crocodile on the Sandbank by Elizabeth Peters
Peters' character Amelia Peabody has been called a female Indiana Jones. This, the first Amelia Peabody mystery, combines mystery, romance, adventure, and humor.

Rebecca by Daphne DuMaurier
This mystery stars no sleuth, just a woman who wants to find out the truth about her husband's first wife.

The Great Train Robbery by Michael Crichton
A mystery with a twist: Crichton reveals just enough to make you wonder how everything will turn out—even though he tells you in the beginning how it does.

The Man Who Was Thursday by G.K. Chesterton
Chesterton's mystery is witty, quirky, and fast-paced.

Action/Adventure
If mysteries are about bringing the wrongdoer to justice, action/adventure stories are about the good guys prevailing—or, in a few cases, surviving. If you're new to this genre, be forewarned that classic adventure stories often have a somewhat slower pace than more contemporary action novels. This list is half classic, half contemporary.

Jurassic Park by Michael Crichton
Crichton is the master of contemporary suspense. Although his books are generally fast-paced, they're also smart—Crichton incorporates a lot of science into his writing. Also consider Crichton's *Congo, Timeline* & *Sphere.*

Around the World in Eighty Days by Jules Verne
A delightful adventure with just the right amount of cleverness and wit.

The Eagle Has Landed by Jack Higgins
Set during World War II, this suspense-filled novel features a daring Nazi plot to kidnap the British Prime Minister –on British soil.

The Princess Bride by William Goldman
Hilarious action tale with just a splash of fantasy and romance.

The Call of the Wild by Jack London
A great story for animal lovers.

Winterdance by Gary Paulsen
Paulsen's memoir of preparing to run the Iditarod is an amazing, laugh out-loud funny, true adventure story.

Shane by Jack Schaefer
A classic cowboy tale. Shane fits the warrior archetype perfectly—students who choose this would benefit from considering how Schaefer uses symbolism.

Treasure Island by Robert Louis Stevenson
Stevenson's action-packed plot moves along briskly—the epitome of an adventure story.

Beat to Quarters by C.S. Forester
Life on an English battleship during the Napoleonic wars: Forester's battle scenes are amazingly detailed and gripping. A&E has adapted Forester's novels into the award-winning Horatio Hornblower series. I recommend both.

Double Identity by Margaret Peterson Haddix
Haddix is a contemporary young adult writer who writes intense and suspenseful plots that deal with thought-provoking themes.

The Hunt for Red October by Tom Clancy
Clancy writes great military suspense. Be forewarned that his stories are quite realistic, so expect some profanity. This is one of his earlier novels.

Fantasy
Fantasy involves realistic characters in an unrealistic world or unrealistic characters in the real world. Other than that, just about anything goes. Fantasy has a shocking number of sub-genres—no list of ten can do them all justice. That being said, I defy anyone to knock my top three fantasy picks.

The Lord of the Rings (trilogy) by J.R.R. Tolkien
Considered by many the greatest literary achievement of the twentieth century. This set (plus *The Hobbit*) belongs on every bookshelf.

Winnie-the-Pooh by A.A. Milne
Ditto for Milne, who is not just for kids! Wonderfully witty, unforgettable characters: Milne's books are full of short stories that everyone can love.

The Chronicles of Narnia (series) by C.S. Lewis
Exciting yet thought-provoking adventures. Also, Lewis' *Screwtape Letters* dishes up a different type of fantasy with more of a theological flavor.

Watership Down by Richard Adams
Epic fantasy about rabbits—hares, actually—learning to live in community. Readers who enjoy *Watership Down* should also consider Adams' less well-known *The Plague Dogs*.

Animal Farm by George Orwell
Social commentary at its best.

The Little Prince by Antoine Saint-Exupery
Lovely tidbits of wisdom. Surprisingly philosophical, but very accessible. Bit of trivia: a friend of mine met Gandhi's personal physician and she said this was her favorite book.

The Chronicles of Prydain (series) by Lloyd Alexander
Similar in some ways to *The Lord of the Rings*, but slightly easier reading.

A Wrinkle in Time (quartet) by Madeleine L'Engle
L'Engle's "affirmation of a universe in which [she] could take note of all the evil and unfairness and horror, and yet believe in a loving Creator" (L'Engle, 2001, p. 136).

The Goose Girl (series) by Shannon Hale
My daughters love these. I believe they're fantasy-slash-romance. For those who like that sort of thing.

Science Fiction Books and Series

Often confused with fantasy, science fiction relies on some creative application of a scientific theory for its premise. A lot (but not all) of it takes place in outer space. I must thank my husband and my daughters for their help in compiling this list, as I am not a great reader of science fiction.

Foundation (series) by Isaac Asimov
Asimov's Foundation insightful series is considered by many to be the best in science fiction. An astonishingly prolific writer, Asimov wrote some 500 books. Consider also reading his *I, Robot* and *Fantastic Voyage* books.

Dune (series) by Frank Hebert
A highly acclaimed, unique epic science fiction series that Arthur C. Clarke compared to *The Lord of the Rings*.

Starship Troopers by Robert Heinlein
Some of Heinlein's writing is not as appropriate for teenagers as this one, but Heinlein is considered one of the genre's masters—definitely classic.

Hitchhiker's Guide to the Galaxy (series) by Douglas Adams
These popular books blend science fiction, fantasy, and humor.

Out of the Silent Planet by C.S. Lewis
The other two books in Lewis' space trilogy aren't as compelling, but this one is good enough to stand alone.

2001: A Space Odyssey by Arthur C. Clarke
One of the more scientifically correct science fiction authors, Clarke chronicles humanity from its beginnings through timelessness.

20,000 Leagues Under the Sea by Jules Verne
The earliest popular science fiction author, Verne developed his first novels based on scrupulously researched science theories way back in the 1860's.

Ender's Game by Orson Scott Card
A militaristic novella with multiple twists, written with a younger audience in mind.

A Connecticut Yankee in King Arthur's Court by Mark Twain
Amusing episodic time-traveling tale by Twain.

The Time Machine by H.G. Wells
One of the first recognized science fiction authors, Wells' writing still holds implications for modern audiences.

Romance

As a genre, romance gets a bad name from all those cheap romance novels they sell in grocery stores—and any work of fiction that is merely romantic probably deserves that reputation. There's nothing cheap, however, about quality romance. Most of the great classic romance stories don't merely bring couples together, they contemplate psychological and especially sociological issues as well. Both *North and South* and *Shirley*, for instance, considered the plight of the lower classes during the English industrial revolution, and *Daniel Deronda* and *Marriage* deal with societal prejudices. Still, what makes most romances so satisfying is the comedic ending, when the couple finally gets together against all odds. A few romantic tragedies round out my list.

Pride and Prejudice by Jane Austen
If you like romance, you'll love Jane Austen. I recommend reading *Northanger Abby* after *Pride and Prejudice*, but all six Austen novels are excellent.

North and South by Elizabeth Gaskell
A "southern" girl moves to England's industrial north and struggles to make sense of the wealth of business owners in light of the hard life of factory workers, and especially in light of John Thornton, who deals justly with his employees. See also Gaskell's *Mary Barton*.

Romeo and Juliet by William Shakespeare
Actually, I prefer Shakespeare's comedy *Much Ado About Nothing*, but this list somehow felt wrong without this title, so here it is.

Gone with the Wind by Margaret Mitchell
A southern belle loves her best friend and sister-in-law's husband, while her third husband loves her but pretends not to. Meanwhile, the Civil War happens and Reconstruction begins. All in all, an amazing historical fiction, psychological and romance novel, rolled into one.

The Importance of Being Earnest by Oscar Wilde
A witty drama with lots of wordplay and silliness—a quick, lighthearted, fun read.

Their Eyes Were Watching God by Zora Neale Hurston
The story of a widowed black woman who marries a younger man in spite of her community's disapproval.

Shirley by Charlotte Brontë
Half sappy romance, half brilliantly instructive. (Worth the sap, though.)

Pygmalion by George Bernard Shaw
A witty and delightful commentary on language and class, Shaw's play comments insightfully on romance as well.

Daniel Deronda by George Eliot
Eliot, who wrote the first multi-plot novel in *Middlemarch*, weaves two plot-lines together in *Daniel Deronda* as well.

Marriage by Susan Ferrier
Ferrier's novel, which travels between London and Scotland, reminds me a little of Jane Austen's writing.

Coming-of-Age

Coming-of-age novels involve a protagonist who grows up. Usually, the main character experiences an epiphany in which he or she grasps some new piece of wisdom about himself or herself or about human nature. This new, more mature way of understanding then propels the character to act in a certain way in order to determine the outcome of events in the novel's climax. Most of the better coming-of-age novels involve somewhat subtle themes that prevent them from feeling preachy or moralistic. Some of the best ones, in my opinion, manage to be both deep and really funny.

Jane Eyre by Charlotte Brontë
Some people take Jane Eyre to be about a woman asserting her independence, but I see Jane learning to discern wisdom through some of the most bizarre dilemmas any woman is likely to ever face—and I do mean, 'bizarre.' Read it and see what you think.

Great Expectations by Charles Dickens
Many people consider this to be Dickens' finest work. I agree—even though Miss Haversham really creeps me out.

I Capture the Castle by Dodie Smith
Sort of a quirky coming-of-age romance conundrum diary novel.

The Outsiders by S.E. Hinton
A modern classic about a boy "from the wrong side of the tracks" trying to make sense of class, conflict, family, and friendship. One of my favorite books as a teen.

Anne of Green Gables (series) by L.M.M. Montgomery

You almost have to like reading to like Anne, but if you do, you'll love her.

Cold Sassy Tree by Olive Burns
Set in the South around the turn of the century, the first-person narrator of this story is the teenaged grandson of a man who re-marries shockingly soon after his first wife's death. The narration is often humorous and sometimes insightful.

The Summer of the Monkeys by Wilson Rawls
The premise is fun: a teenaged boy determines to catch a troop of runaway circus monkeys so he can buy himself a horse. The protagonist's epiphany in this novel is perfect.

Jacob I Have Loved by Katherine Patterson
Every kid feels unappreciated sometimes—well, at least, I think most kids do. This story explores the feelings of a girl whose twin sister seems to have gotten all the grace in the family and captures what it means for her to finally grow up.

Bambi by Felix Salten
This anthropomorphic coming-of-age story is a timeless tale that's not just for children.

Daisy Fay and the Miracle Man by Fannie Flagg
Daisy Fay is one of the funniest narrators ever. This title gets my recommendation because of the unforgettable narrator's first-person voice.

Autobiography/Biography/Memoir
Autobiographies, biographies, and memoirs are the most fiction-like books in all of nonfiction. Some of these books tell about individuals who lived through extraordinary experiences, while others describe individuals who were themselves extraordinary; still others tell about ordinary experiences exceptionally well. Although it's nearly impossible to recommend just a few, I've tried to maintain variety in these suggestions.

The Hiding Place by Corrie Ten Boom
The autobiographical account of a Dutch woman who hid Jews in her home during WWII. It captures living truthfully in a beautiful and powerful way.

The Diary of Anne Frank by Anne Frank
The diary of a Jewish girl hiding from Nazis in an attic—kind of the flip side of *The Hiding Place*.

Inside the Third Reich by Albert Speer
Written by Hitler's architect, a man who technically did nothing wrong—except, that is, prolonging Hitler's success. Challenging, thought-provoking book.

Incidents in the Life of a Slave Girl by Harriet Jacobs
Bearing some similarity to Anne Frank's situation, in this autobiographical memoir, a former slave hides in an attic for seven years to evade capture.

Apollo 13 by Jim Lovell and Jeffrey Kluger
This memoir of Jim Lovell describes the defunct mission of Apollo 13.

Animals in Translation by Temple Grandin
Half about understanding animals, half about understanding autism, there's something of interest on every page.

Boy & Going Solo by Roald Dahl
The author of *Charlie and the Chocolate Factory* writes about his youth. Great and relatively easy-to-read stories about growing up about a hundred years ago.

Catch Me If You Can by Frank Abagnale (with Stan Redding)
Fast-paced account of a swindler and impersonator. Thankfully, Mr. Abagnale has changed his ways.

Cheaper By the Dozen by Frank Gilbreth, Jr. and Ernestine Gilbreth Carey
A humorous account of family life.

World History, Historical Fiction and Sociological Works

I'm lumping a few different types of books here: history, which tells what happened; historical fiction, which tells a story that happens during a particular period of history; and sociological fiction, which are books which were historically important because they challenged societal values. Although not quite the same, all of the books below vividly depict what life was like for people who lived through a particular situation or period in history or historical event. Most of the books below ponder complex issues and develop thought-provoking themes.

All Quiet on the Western Front by Eric Maria Remarque
Remarque's Paul reminds us that even the enemy is human. Written with humor and pathos, this is a beautiful book, despite its context of war.

Things Fall Apart by Chinua Achebe
Achebe helps readers understand what it would have been like to be evangelized by white people without romanticizing the native culture.

Cry, the Beloved Country by Alan Paton
Beautiful, heart-breaking, and inspiring story about a rural South African pastor who goes searching for his missing family members in Johannesburg. Confronted by the realities of apartheid, the pastor encounters much injustice but also finds grace in the actions of people who show generosity and compassion.

A Night to Remember by Walter Lord
Historical account of the night the Titanic sank—reads like fast-paced fiction. Also, consider Lord's *Day of Infamy*—the definitive account of the attack on Pearl Harbor by the Japanese.

Band of Brothers by Stephen Ambrose
Both Ambrose's history and the HBO miniseries produced by Tom Hanks and Steven Spielberg will evoke gratitude for the soldiers who fought in WWII.

To Kill a Mockingbird by Harper Lee
One of those books that everyone should read. Wonderfully readable story with likeable characters and a rich theme.

The Education of Little Tree by Forester Carter
Poignant, sometimes funny story of an orphan raised by Cherokee grandparents.

Mila 18 by Leon Uris
Uris depicts the resilient Polish and Jewish families who fought against Nazi humiliation, deprivation, and extermination in WWII.

The Dollmaker by Harriet Arnow
Gertie Nevels yearns to own a small farm in Kentucky, but when her husband takes a job in a Detroit factory during World War II, she and their five children follow him north and discover prejudice and injustice—and friends and kindness.

The Good Earth by Pearl Buck
A novel about a poor Chinese man who eventually gains wealth—but at what cost?

A Passage to India by E.M. Forster
An English woman journeys to India and discovers her own unconscious prejudice.

One Day in the Life of Ivan Denisovich by Alexander Solzhenitsyn
Depicts life in a Russian prison camp.

Uncle Tom's Cabin by Harriet Beecher Stowe
The classic novel that galvanized the abolitionist movement before the Civil War.

All the President's Men by Carl Bernstein and Bob Woodward
Riveting exposé of corruption in the Nixon White House.

O! Pioneers by Willa Cather
Cather's book reminds me of *Little House on the Prairie*, only more grown up.

Black Odyssey: The Case of the Slave Ship 'Amistad' by Mary Cable
A group of kidnapped Africans gain control of their slave ship and mutiny; later, when their right to freedom is challenged in court, John Quincy Adams defends the would-be slaves.

The Jungle by Upton Sinclair
A muckraker's account of life for immigrants recruited to work in the meat-packing industry. Tragic, but powerful.

Short Story Collections and Novellas
Stocking short stories allows students to sample genres and authors without investing too much time. Short stories capture their themes with an economy of words. Dover Publications offers a number of inexpensive collections of short stories. Here are a few collections that I would recommend.

The Complete Short Stories of Mark Twain by Mark Twain
Many of Twain's short stories are hilarious.

Enter Jeeves: 15 Early Stories by P.G. Wodehouse
Wodehouse was one of the great humorists of the 20th century.

The Best of Sherlock Holmes by Sir Arthur Conan Doyle
The classic mysteries.

Tales from the Perilous Realm by J.R.R. Tolkien
See also the short stories of George MacDonald for more short fantasy.

Isaac Asimov: The Complete Short Stories (Volume I) by Isaac Asimov
For those who wish to sample some science fiction, Asimov can't be beat.

Brave Companions: Portraits in History by David McCullough
These biographical essays inform readers about several often overlooked but historically important individuals.

The Uncommon Reader by Alan Bennett (novella)
A humorous novella in which the Queen of England discovers the public library.

The Old Man and the Sea by Ernest Hemingway (novella)
Hemingway's novella is his most popular work for teens, possibly because some of his novels can be rather grim and sometimes offensive.

The Pearl by John Steinbeck (novella)
A well-written Mexican folktale with a sound moral for adolescents. Like Hemingway, Steinbeck wrote novels that some readers found offensive.

A Christmas Carol by Charles Dickens (novella)
The best introduction to Dickens, conveniently brief and familiar.

Video Adaptations

So many classic titles are available on DVD these days, I'm almost at a loss to make any claims here at all. Still, I can tell you what we've seen and enjoyed, and by no means did we enjoy all of the classic films I stuck in a DVD player and turned on, hoping my girls wouldn't notice they were being edified. The following movies, however, we all enjoyed. In fact, some of them rank among our favorite movies.

Productions of Shakespeare's Plays: Kenneth Branagh's film adaptations of Shakespeare's works: *Henry V, As You Like It, Love's Labour Lost,* and *Much Ado About Nothing,* also Trevor Nunn's adaptation of *Twelfth Night* and BBC Warner's 2010 adaptation of *Hamlet*

Adaptations of the Novels of Jane Austen: A&E's 1995 adaptation of *Pride and Prejudice,* Ang Lee's version of *Sense and Sensibility,* Masterpiece Theater's 2008 *Northanger Abbey,* and either the shorter 1996 adaptation of *Emma* starring Gwyneth Paltrow or the longer 2009 BBC version starring Romola Garai

BBC's adaptations of Elizabeth Gaskell's *North and South, Wives and Daughters,* and *Cranford*

The 2002 adaptation of Oscar Wilde's *The Importance of Being Earnest*

The 1989 mini-series adaptation of Jules Vernes' *Around the World in 80 Days*

A&E's Jeeves and Wooster series starring Stephen Fry and Hugh Laurie

The 1985 Sherlock Holmes Collection starring Jeremy Brett

A&E's Horatio Hornblower series adapts the novels of C.S. Forester.

The 1964 musical "My Fair Lady" is an adaptation of George Bernard Shaw's *Pygmalion.*

Great Book Authors

The list that follows, though far from exhaustive, includes authors and books that others have considered truly great. By the time a high school student completes the four-year program, he or she should have sampled at least a few works written by one or more of the authors listed below.

Epic/Poetry/Drama
[The Old Testament]
[The New Testament]
William Shakespeare
Homer
Virgil
Sophocles
Dante Alighieri
John Milton
Henry Ibsen
George Bernard Shaw

Philosophy (Economics,
Education, Ethics, & Politics)
Aristotle
Plato
Jean Jacques Rousseau
Adam Smith
Charles de Secondat, Baron de
Montesquieu
Alexander Hamilton, John Jay,
and James Madison
Alexis de Tocqueville
Henry David Thoreau
John Dewey

Mathematics/Science
Aristotle
Charles Darwin
Rene Descartes
Albert Einstein
Euclid
Michael Faraday
Galileo Galilei
Johannes Kepler
Antoine Laurent Lavoisier
Isaac Newton

Novelists
Jane Austen
Daniel Defoe
Charles Dickens
Fyodor Dostoevsky
George Eliot
Gustave Flaubert
Nathaniel Hawthorne
Herman Melville
Leo Tolstoy
Mark Twain

CLASSIC LITERATURE

CATEGORIZED BY DIFFICULTY AND LENGTH

The purpose of this list is to help you sort out which classic literary works are best suited to your student's level of ability. This list categorizes literary works that have endured for at least forty years by the level of challenge each presents, based on each work's Lexile measure and, to a lesser extent, its length.

Though Level 1 books are the easiest works on these lists, they're not particularly easy; they are more or less equivalent in terms of reading difficulty to many popular, contemporary fiction works such those written by Michael Crichton, Stephanie Meyer, or James Patterson. Also, the books identified in Levels 11 and 12 reflect a greater range of difficulty than other levels. These books represent some of the hardest books anyone might encounter.

Length is indicated by the number in parentheses following each title. A one indicates short stories of less than 50 pages and a two represents novellas of around 100 pages, while a six indicates more than 750 pages and a seven over 1000. Although this list is neither exhaustive nor is my categorization exactly precise (the different font sizes in books affects the length factor), it should give you some idea of which books will be most appropriate to your student's reading ability and stamina. Where multiple books (series, trilogy, quartet) are indicated, the length indicator reflects the average length of each book in the grouping; in books that contain collections of essays or short stories, the number reflects the length of each individual unit.

Unlike the list of recommendations in the previous section, I have not read all of the books on this list, so I can't vouch for all of the content in these books. I have, however, excluded a few titles that you might have expected to find here that I have read and considered inappropriate for young readers. Among these are a few otherwise worthy titles. Alex Haley's *Roots*, for instance, is an amazing literary achievement, but it does contain a few tragic scenes that must disturb any reader, but might especially alarm adolescents. Such works, in my opinion, are better encountered as mature adults.

In general, assume that literature published more than a century ago does not include disturbing or offensive content; among books published after World War I, this assumption may not always hold. It's always a good idea to forewarn students to run a book by you if the content in it seems iffy to them.

Level 1 Classics (Easiest)

The Fantastic Voyage (3) and *The Fantastic Voyage II* (3) by Isaac Asimov
The Martian Chronicles (3) by Ray Bradbury
Wuthering Heights (3) by Emily Brontë
Secret of the Andes (3) by Ann Clark
The Black Stallion (3) by Walter Farley
A Room with a View (3) by E.M. Forster
The Lord of the Flies (3) by William Golding
The Sun Also Rises (3) by Ernest Hemingway
The Outsiders (3) and *That was Then, This is Now* (3) by S.E. Hinton
Young Pioneers (3) by Rose Wilder Lane
The Wrinkle in Time quartet (3) by Madeleine L'Engle
Winnie the Pooh (1) and *The House at Pooh Corner* (1) by A.A. Milne
Gentle Ben (3) by Walt Morey
Where the Red Fern Grows (3) by Wilson Rawls
Bambi (3) by Felix Sarten
The Little Prince (2) by Antoine Saint-Exupery
Call it Courage (2) by Armstrong Sperry
Of Mice and Men (2) and *The Red Pony* (1) by John Steinbeck
The Strange Case of Dr. Jekyll and Mr. Hyde (2) by Robert Louis Stevenson
Night (2) by Elie Wiesel

Level 2 Classics

Things Fall Apart (3) by Chinua Achebe
National Velvet (3) by Enid Bagnold
The Last Unicorn (3) by Peter Beagle
Fahrenheit 561 (3) by Ray Bradbury
The Stranger (3) by Albert Camus
Murder on the Orient Express (3) by Agatha Christie
The Ox-Bow Incident (3) by Walter Clark
The Autobiography of Miss Jane Pittman (3) by Ernest Gaines
Cheaper by the Dozen (3) by Frank Gilbreth, Jr. & Ernestine Gilbreth Carey
Old Yeller (2) by Fred Gipson
The Old Man and the Sea (2) by Ernest Hemingway
The Legend of Sleepy Hollow and *Rip Van Winkle* (1) by Washington Irving
Incidents in the Life of a Slave Girl (3) by Harriet Jacobs
The Phantom Tollbooth (3) by Norton Juster
Lassie Come Home (3) by Eric Knight
Shane (3) by Jack Schaefer
Bronze Bow (3) and *The Witch of Blackbird Pond* (3) by Elizabeth George Speare

Daughter of Time (3) by Josephine Tey
Macho (3) by Edmund Villaseñor

Level 3 Classics
The Chronicles of Prydain series (3) by Lloyd Alexander
I, Robot (3) by Isaac Asimov
A Little Princess (3) by Frances Burnett
Alice in Wonderland (3) by Lewis Carroll
O! Pioneers (3) by Willa Cather
A Christmas Carol (2) by Charles Dickens
Johnny Tremain (4) by Esther Forbes
The Stout-Hearted Seven (3) by Neta Lohnes Frazier
Black Like Me (3) by John Howard Griffin
Siddhartha (2) by Hermann Hesse
No Promises in the Wind (3) by Irene Hunt
The Turn of the Screw (3) by Henry James
Flowers for Algernon (3) by Daniel Keyes
To Kill a Mockingbird (3) by Harper Lee
The Narnia Chronicles (3) by C.S. Lewis
White Fang (3) by Jack London
A Night to Remember (3) by Walter Lord
The Heart is a Lonely Hunter (4) by Carson McCullers
Tales of the South Pacific (4) by James Michener
Cry, the Beloved Country (4) by Alan Paton
All Quiet on the Western Front (3) by Erich Maria Remarque
Strong Poison (3) by Dorothy Sayers
Black Beauty (3) by Anna Sewell
One Day in the Life of Ivan Denisovich (3) by Alexander Solzhenitsyn
The Grapes of Wrath (5) and *The Pearl* (1) by John Steinbeck
The Adventures of Tom Sawyer (3) by Mark Twain
The Time Machine (3) by H.G. Wells
Ethan Frome (2) by Edith Wharton

Level 4 Classics
Watership Down (4) by Richard Adams
Foundation series (4) by Isaac Asimov
The Secret Garden (3) by Frances Burnett
The Dark is Rising series (3) by Susan Cooper
The Red Badge of Courage (3) by Stephen Crane
Rebecca (4) by Daphne Du Maurier
As I Lay Dying (4) by William Faulkner

Howard's End (4) by E.M. Forster
The Power and the Glory (3) by Graham Greene
The House of the Seven Gables (4) by Nathaniel Hawthorne
For Whom the Bell Tolls (4) by Ernest Hemingway
Captains Courageous (3) and *Kim* (4) by Rudyard Kipling
The Laird's Inheritance (3) by George MacDonald
Anne of Green Gables series (3) by L.M. Montgomery
My Friend Flicka (4) by Mary O'Hara
The Yearling (5) by Marjorie Rawlings
The Story of an African Farm (3) by Olive Schreiner
A Tree Grows in Brooklyn (4) by Betty Smith
I Capture the Castle (4) by Dodie Smith
Calico Captive (3) by Elizabeth George Speare
Heidi (3) by Johanna Spyri
The Hiding Place (3) by Corrie ten Boom
The Lord of the Rings trilogy (4) by J.R.R.Tolkien
Rebecca of Sunnybrook Farm (3) by Kate Douglas Wiggins

Level 5 Classics
The Wizard of Oz (2) by Frank Baum
Stampede for Gold (3) by Pierre Berton
The Man Who Was Thursday (3) by G.K. Chesterton
The Heart of Darkness (3) by Joseph Conrad
A Tale of Two Cities (3) by Charles Dickens
A Narrative of the Life of Frederick Douglass (3) by Frederick Douglass
2001: A Space Odyssey (3) by Arthur Clarke
The Great Gatsby (3) by F. Scott Fitzgerald
Death Be Not Proud (3) by John Gunther
Starship Troopers (3) by Robert Heinlein
Their Eyes Were Watching God (3) by Zora Neale Hurston
Brave New World (3) by Aldous Huxley
Out of the Silent Planet (3) by C.S. Lewis
The Call of the Wild (2) by Jack London
Day of Infamy (3) by Walter Lord
The Princess and the Goblin (3) by George MacDonald
Frankenstein (3) by Mary Shelley
Kidnapped (4) by Robert Louis Stevenson
The Adventures of Huckleberry Finn (3) by Mark Twain
Around the World in 80 Days (3) by Jules Verne
The Invisible Man (3) by H.G. Wells
Our Town and other plays (2) by Thornton Wilder

The Bridge of San Luis Rey (2) by Thornton Wilder

<u>Level 6</u>
Jane Eyre (4) and *Shirley* (4) by Charlotte Brontë
Pilgrim's Progress (4) by John Bunyan
My Antonia (3) by Willa Cather
Hans Brinker or the Silver Skates (3) by Mary Dodge
The Man in the Iron Mask (4) and *The Three Musketeers* (4) by Alexandre Dumas
Madame Bovary (3) and *Three Tales* (1) by Gustave Flaubert
A Passage to India (4) by E.M. Forster
Adam of the Road (4) by Elizabeth Gray
Mythology (4) by Edith Hamilton
Return of the Native (4) by Thomas Hardy
Beowulf (3) translated by Seamus Heaney
Dune series (5) by Frank Hebert
Stranger in a Strange Land (4) by Robert Heinlein
All Creatures Great and Small (4) by James Herriot
A Canticle for Liebowitz (4) by Walter Miller
Emily of New Moon series (4) and *Rilla of Ingleside* (3) by L.M. Montgomery
Lad: A Dog (3) by Albert Terhune
The Hobbit (3) by J.R.R.Tolkien
The Death of Ivan Ilych (2) by Leo Tolstoy
Ben Hur (4) by Lew Wallace
Jeeves Takes Charge (1) by P.G. Wodehouse
All the President's Men (4) by Bob Woodward and Carl Bernstein
To the Lighthouse (3) by Virginia Woolf

<u>Level 7 Classics</u>
Born Free by (3) Joy Adamson
Pere Goriot (3) by Honoré Balzac
Black Odyssey: Case of the Slave Ship Amistad (3) by Mary Cable
I, Juan de Pareja (3) by Elizabeth Borton deTrevino
Oliver Twist (4) by Charles Dickens
The Adventures of Sherlock Holmes (1) by Arthur Conan Doyle
The Hound of the Baskervilles (3) by Arthur Conan Doyle
Jamaica Inn (4) by Daphne Du Maurier
Barbary Pirates (3) by C.S. Forester
The Diary of Anne Frank (3) by Anne Frank
The Wind in the Willows (3) by Kenneth Grahame
The Mayor of Casterbridge (3) by Thomas Hardy
Hiroshima (3) by John Hersey

Across Five Aprils (3) by Irene Hunt
The Jungle Book (3) by Rudyard Kipling
The Princess and Curdie (3) by George MacDonald
Invincible Louisa (3) by Cornelia Meigs
1984 (3) and *Animal Farm* (2) by George Orwell
Pygmalion (2) and other plays by George Bernard Shaw
Gulliver's Travels (3) by Jonathan Swift
Civil Disobedience (2) by Henry David Thoreau
The Warden (3) by Anthony Trollope
A Connecticut Yankee in King Arthur's Court (3) by Mark Twain
Pudd'nhead Wilson (3) and *The Prince and the Pauper* (3) by Mark Twain
Mila 18 (5) by Leon Uris
The War of the Worlds (2) by H.G. Wells
The Importance of Being Earnest (2) and other plays by Oscar Wilde

Level 8 Classics
Northanger Abbey (3) and *Persuasion* (3) by Jane Austen
Pride and Prejudice (3) and *Sense and Sensibility* (3) by Jane Austen
Bury My Heart at Wounded Knee (4) by Dee Brown
The Incredible Journey (3) by Sheila Burnford
Tarzan of the Apes (3) by Edgar Burroughs
Death Comes for the Archbishop (4) by Willa Cather
The Scarlet Pimpernel (4) by Baroness D'Orczy
Crime and Punishment (5) by Fyodor Dostoyevsky
The Lost World (3) by Arthur Conan Doyle
African Queen (3) by C.S. Forester
Beat to Quarters (3) and the Horatio Hornblower series by C.S. Forester
Cranford (3) and *Mary Barton* (4) by Elizabeth Gaskell
Tess of the D'Urbervilles (4) by Thomas Hardy
With Lee in Virginia (4) and other titles by G.A. Henty
The Odyssey (3) by Homer
A Portrait of a Lady (4) by Henry James
The Metamorphosis by (1) Franz Kafka
The Trumpeter of Krakow (3) by Eric Kelly
Sea Wolf (4) by Jack London
Christy (5) by Catherine Marshall
George Washington: Frontier Colonel (3) by Sterling North
The Jungle (4) by Upton Sinclair
Treasure Island (3) by Robert Louis Stevenson
Uncle Tom's Cabin (4) by Harriet Beecher Stowe
The Silmarillion (4) by J.R.R. Tolkien

Exodus (5) by Leon Uris
Twenty Thousand Leagues Under the Sea (4) by Jules Verne
The Sword in the Stone (3) by T. H. White

Level 9 Classics
The Dollmaker (5) by Harriet Arnow
Emma (4) and *Mansfield Park* (4) by Jane Austen
The Bridge over the River Kwai (3) by Pierre Boulle
The Moonstone (5) by Wilkie Collins
Robinson Crusoe (3) by Daniel Defoe
The Count of Monte Cristo (6) by Alexandre Dumas
Silas Marner (3) by George Eliot
Marriage (4) by Susan Ferrier
The Story of my Experiments with Truth (5) by Mohandas Karamchand Gandhi
The Dark Frigate (3) by Charles Hawes
A Prayer for Owen Meany (5) by John Irving
The Autobiography of Benjamin Franklin (3) by Benjamin Franklin
Babbitt (4) and *Main Street* (5) by Sinclair Lewis
Never Cry Wolf (3) by Farley Mowat
Doctor Zhivago (5) by Boris Pasternak
The Adventures of Robin Hood (4) by Howard Pyle
All the King's Men (5) by Robert Penn Warren
The Swiss Family Robinson (4) by Johann Wyss

Level 10 Classics
Little Women (4) by Louisa May Alcott
The Good Earth (4) by Pearl Buck
Erewhon (3) by Samuel Butler
Silent Spring by (4) Rachel Carson
The Last of the Mohicans (4) by James Fenimore Cooper
David Copperfield (7) and *Great Expectations* (4) by Charles Dickens
The Old Curiosity Shop (4) by Charles Dickens
Out of Africa (4) by Isak Dinesen
The Brothers Karamazov (5) and *The Idiot* (5) by Fyodor Dostoyevsky
Adam Bede (5), *The Mill on the Floss* (4), and *Middlemarch* (5) by George Eliot
North and South (4) and *Wives and Daughters* (5) by Elizabeth Gaskell
I, Claudius (4) by Robert Graves
The Scarlet Letter (3) by Nathaniel Hawthorne
Catch-22 (5) by Joseph Heller
The Iliad (4) by Homer
Notre Dame de Paris (5) by Victor Hugo

Billy Budd (3) and *Moby Dick* (5) by Herman Melville
Gone with the Wind (7) by Margaret Mitchell
Out of My Life and Thought (4) by Albert Schweitzer
A Midsummer's Night's Dream (2); *Twelfth Night* (2); *The Taming of the Shrew* (3);
The Merchant of Venice (2); *As You Like It* (2); *Much Ado About Nothing* (2);
Richard II (3); *Richard III* (3); *Henry IV, Part One* (3); *Henry IV, Part Two* (3); *Henry V*
(3); *Romeo and Juliet* (3); *Hamlet* (3); *Othello* (3); *King Lear* (3); *Julius Caesar* (2);
MacBeth (2) and other plays by William Shakespeare
Phineas Finn (5) by Anthony Trollope
The Aeneid (4) by Vergil
The House of Mirth (4) by Edith Wharton

Level 11
Moll Flanders (4) by Daniel Defoe
Daniel Deronda (6) by George Eliot
Tom Jones (6) by Henry Fielding
One Hundred Years of Solitude (4) by Gabriel Garcia Marquez
The History and Decline and Fall of Roman Empire (6) by Edward Gibbons
Les Miserables (7) by Victor Hugo
The History of Rasselas, Prince of Abissinia (3) by Samuel Johnson
The Social Contract (2) by Jean Jacques Rousseau
The Agony and the Ecstasy (6) by Irving Stone
A Modest Proposal (2) by Jonathan Swift
Vanity Fair (6) by William Makepeace Thackeray
Anna Karenina (5) and *War and Peace* (7) by Leo Tolstoy
Walden (3) by Henry David Thoreau

Level 12 (most difficult)
Don Quixote (6) by Miguel de Cervantes
The Canterbury Tales (5) by Geoffrey Chaucer
The Divine Comedy (5) by Alighieri Dante
The Origin of Species (6) by Charles Darwin
Relativity: The Special and General Theory (3) by Albert Einstein
The Federalist (5) by Alexander Hamilton, John Jay, and James Madison
The Betrothed (5) by Alessandro Manzoni
Ivanhoe (4) by Sir William Scott
The Wealth of Nations (5) by Adam Smith
Democracy in America (5) by Alexis de Tocqueville

LEARNING CONTRACTS

TEACHER PLANNING WORKSHEET

Instructions: Use this worksheet to think about what options you wish to offer your student by marking options that might be helpful to your student. Remember, these suggestions are offered to help you individualize requirements for each student, so not all suggestions will be helpful in all cases: a suggestion that facilitates growth for one student may hinder another. For instance, a slow reader may benefit from reading along to audio texts, while the same strategy might actually slow a fluent reader. A very low minimum requirement for reading projects may free an ambitious student to take on *War and Peace*, while a reluctant student may take advantage of that freedom to take it easy.

How will your requirements allow your student to make significant choices?

☐   Require significantly fewer projects than the student is capable of completing

☐   Make relatively few demands regarding reading from different genres or classic texts

☐   Allow the student to choose the main focus of the course (i.e., a focus on fantasy) and have the student agree to your set of requirements ensuring growth

How will your requirements help your student expand his or her reading selections?

☐   Require the student to experiment with a certain number of different authors

☐   Require the student to experiment with a certain number of different genres

☐   Require the student to read works from different periods (classic, modern classic, contemporary)

What activities will help your student to accelerate his or her reading speed?

☐   Re-reading previously read favorites

☐   Reading literary works of an easier level of difficulty

☐   Reading literary works that are appealing in terms of taste or interest

☐   Reading shorter works like short stories, poems, dramas, and essays

How will your requirements motivate your student to read something longer or harder than he or she normally would choose?

☐ Require students to read a certain number of classics

☐ Permit students to fulfill a requirement for more difficult reading with a short story, novella, or essay

☐ Permit students to watch a video adaptation before reading the text

☐ Permit students to fulfill two reading projects by reading works of more than 400 pages

☐ Set no requirement for number of reading projects so long as student reads for at least an hour daily

How will your requirements permit your student to take a mental break with a fun or light choice from time to time?

☐ Stock some appealing but tasteful contemporary fiction

☐ Stock books from light-hearted genres such as humor or comics (if your student studies a foreign language, comic strips in that language are often a fun option)

☐ Stock books of various lengths and levels of difficulty

How will your requirements help your student to accumulate a significant number of experiences with recognizable literary classics?

☐ Require the student to read a certain number of classic works

☐ Permit alternative activities such as listening to audio versions and reading along

☐ Accept watching video adaptations of classic literary works in lieu of some of the requirements for reading

How will your requirements ensure documentation of student work?

☐ Require the student to log and rate books

☐ Require the student to complete worksheets

☐ Require the student to summarize literary works

☐ Require the student to write book reviews

☐ Require the student to write a literary analysis or literary reflection

LEARNING CONTRACT

Student_____ Semester_____

Instructions: Select one option from each column. Abiding by the learning content option that you choose, read or work on learning products for at least one hour daily or five hours each week.

Learning Content	Learning Process	Learning Product

Submit all completed products by_____
Signature of Teacher _____
Signature of Student _____

READING LOG

Student   Semester

Date	Author	Title	Genre	Classic?	Rating

HOW TO DESIGNATE RATINGS

5 = You love it. You intend to read it again, maybe often. You like the book so much that you recommend it to all of your friends.

4 = You really liked it. You intend to read it again someday. If a friend asked you if you would recommend it, you would say, "Yeah, it's pretty good."

3= You like it okay. You don't think you'll want to read it again, but it was good enough that you never thought about giving up on it. If a friend asked you if you would recommend it, you would say, "Maybe. It depends on what you like."

2 = You don't like it. Not only would you never read it again, you weren't sure you wanted to finish the first time. If a friend asked if you would recommend the book, you would say, "No."

1 = You hate it. You maybe couldn't even finish it. It was so bad that it actually offended you. You go out of your way to warn your friends not to read it.

LITERARY GENRES REFERENCE PAGE

I. Poetry

II. Nonfiction

    A.   Opinionated essays (sometimes called op-eds) reveal someone's opinions about a subject

    B.   Autobiography, biography, and memoir tell you about a real person's life. Autobiographies are fairly all-encompassing accounts of the life of the author; memoirs usually focus on a particular time period or aspect of a person's life. Biographies tell an individual's life story but are written by another person.

    C.   History describes historical events as they occurred; it includes many facts.

    D.   Informational books transmit knowledge and explain concepts.

    E.   Instructional or How-to books explain how to do something.

III. Drama (plays)

IV. Fiction

    A.   Mystery involves discovering the truth about something, usually a crime.

    B.   Suspense/thriller involves people trying to survive dangerous situations.

    C.   Horror usually involves people pitted against supernatural threats.

    D.   Action/Adventure involves people experiencing unusual and exciting situations that may be dangerous, but usually danger is limited to specific episodes (as opposed to thrillers, where the danger remains intense right up to the end).

    E.   Science Fiction involves imaginative applications of science and technology.

    F.   Fantasy involves realistic characters in imaginary settings or imaginary characters in realistic settings.

    G.   Romance involves two individuals either finding love or losing it.

    H.   Coming-of-Age involves the wisdom a person gains through maturing.

    I.   Historical Fiction sets a story and characters in realistic historical periods.

    J.   Literary Fiction usually features vivid description and well-developed characters but weak plots and ambiguous themes.

    K.   Sociological books make a point about an issue affecting society in general.

    L.   Psychological books focus on the way characters think and feel.

    M.   Short Stories compress narrative elements into few words; many contemporary short stories are more literary and lack clear resolutions and themes.

STRUCTURAL ELEMENTS IN FICTION

The worksheets in this section consist of checklists that should take students minutes to complete. These checklists are teaching tools, providing brief definitions for the literary terms students will need in order to discuss and analyze fiction intelligibly on future assignments. Most students will rapidly familiarize themselves with the terminology provided and soon be able to skim over the checklists, marking off the appropriate choices rapidly.

Structural Elements in Fiction: Plots

Rating ☐

Title/Author _____

The best genre category for this book is:

- ☐ Mystery (the protagonist discovers the hidden truth about something)
- ☐ Suspense/thriller (the protagonist struggles to escape or survive)
- ☐ Action/adventure (the protagonist ventures out on a quest for treasure, fun, or fame)
- ☐ Romantic comedy (the events lead to a couple coming together)
- ☐ Coming-of-age (a young protagonist matures and grows wiser through events)
- ☐ Historical fiction (events take place during a specific period in history)
- ☐ Sociological (the story concerns people seeking justice or living in oppression)
- ☐ Psychological (the climax involves the protagonist making a personal decision)
- ☐ Literary (characters and description are strong, but plot is weak; climax is ambiguous)

The plot develops mostly because of the conflict between the protagonist and:

- ☐ the antagonist (a character who competes with the protagonist or otherwise prevents him or her from achieving his or her main goal)
- ☐ a group of people, an organization, or society in general
- ☐ nature (the protagonist must survive, pitted against the forces of nature)
- ☐ him/herself (the book is mainly about a character deliberating between two choices)

The climax was obvious because that was when:

- ☐ the culprit or truth was revealed
- ☐ the antagonist or bad-guy/evil empire was defeated
- ☐ the protagonist saved the day
- ☐ the protagonist survived the threat
- ☐ the protagonist understood something new
- ☐ the protagonist's desire was finally fulfilled
- ☐ something happened that changed everything
- ☐ the climax was hard to pick out

The plot (or the sequence of events) in this book is:

- ☐ unified—events mostly lead up to the book's climax
- ☐ episodic—the events seem like separate stories that don't all lead up to a single climax
- ☐ multiple—several plot-lines with different main characters converge late in the book

The pacing for the plot was:

- ☐ fast—the story had lots of action and brisk dialogue
- ☐ average—somewhere in between fast and slow
- ☐ slow: the narrator meticulously describes the setting and characters; some characters make speeches

Structural Elements in Fiction: Characterization

Rating ☐

Title/Author _____

The POV (point-of-view) in the book is:
- ☐ 1st person (the narrator—usually the protagonist—refers to him/herself as "I")
- ☐ 3rd person, single perspective (the story tells you the main character's perspective only)
- ☐ 3rd person, multiple (different people's perspectives are told at different points)
- ☐ 3rd person, objective (only the action is described; no thoughts are revealed)
- ☐ Omniscient (the narrator has unlimited knowledge of everyone's thoughts and everything that happens)

The author makes the main character seem "round," like a real, complex person by:
- ☐ revealing character's thoughts
- ☐ giving the main character's flaws or weaknesses
- ☐ using backstory, or revealing what happened to the character before the story started
- ☐ balancing the character's good and bad traits
- ☐ giving the character a sense of humor

Is the main character, or protagonist, more of a:
- ☐ static character, whom the events don't change in any significant way
- ☐ developing character, who learns to think or behave differently due to the events that take place in the story

Is the antagonist—the character who opposes the protagonist—mostly:
- ☐ flat—the character is totally good or bad, not quite like a normal person
- ☐ round—the character has a personality with strengths and weaknesses and seems real
- ☐ static—who doesn't learn or change through the course of events
- ☐ developing—he or she learns something due to the events that take place in the story

Secondary characters in the story serve which of the following purposes:
- ☐ help the protagonist achieve his or her goals
- ☐ seem to want to help but actually frustrate the protagonist's ultimate desire or goal
- ☐ seem to oppose the protagonist but end up helping him or her in the end
- ☐ neither help nor hinder much but mostly provide comic relief for the story

Is the denouement—or the way the story turns out—primarily:
- ☐ comedic: the good characters are rewarded and the bad characters punished
- ☐ tragic: the protagonist's efforts go awry; the protagonist's hopes are disappointed
- ☐ ambiguous: whether the final outcome is positive isn't entirely clear

Structural Elements in Fiction: Character Development

Rating ☐

Title/Author _____

In the beginning of the narrative, the protagonist :
- ☐ is doing okay; the main character is looking forward to good things
- ☐ is feeling melancholy because life has become boring or hopeless
- ☐ thinks things are going okay, but in fact, the character has stopped growing as a person
- ☐ thinks things are worse than they really are and needs a new perspective
- ☐ has a serious moral or social problem that is hurting other people

What changes things?
- ☐ A new character arrives and shakes things up.
- ☐ A familiar character changes or moves away.
- ☐ The protagonist's situation suddenly changes due to forces beyond his or her control.
- ☐ The protagonist gets a wonderful opportunity or accepts a challenge.

How does the protagonist deal with problems in the novel? (For instance, does the main character always try to solve problems alone instead of asking for help from friends? Does the character always run away from problems instead of facing them or look for someone else to blame?)
- ☐ He or she uses the same strategy to deal with problems in the beginning and end.
- ☐ He or she changes strategies for dealing with problems from the beginning to the end.
- ☐ He or she keeps trying different strategies for dealing with problems.

The protagonist learns about his or her flaws through:
- ☐ an epiphany—a moment where the character realizes something that he or she never understood before
- ☐ a situation that simply won't resolve, no matter what the character tries to fix it
- ☐ another character, who tells the main character the truth about himself or herself, maybe in anger
- ☐ another situation that the character suddenly realizes is like his or her own situation

In the climax, does the protagonist:
- ☐ make a decision that shows that he's or she's overcome that flaw and has grown?
- ☐ act in a way that he or she never would have before, possibly for someone else's sake?
- ☐ risk everything?
- ☐ redefine himself or herself?

Structural Elements in Fiction: Setting

Rating ☐

Title/Author _____

Do the events in this story take place:
- ☐ mainly within a specific location such as a particular house, city, forest, or realm
- ☐ along the way as the protagonist moves from one location to another
- ☐ along the way as the protagonist journeys to and from a destination
- ☐ someplace where the protagonist doesn't normally belong and has to adapt

Does the story take place in or on any of the following:
- ☐ Ocean or outer space (both exciting and expansive but also very dangerous places)
- ☐ Island (a compressed place where people can create a utopia—or a dystopia)
- ☐ Desert or ice (desolate places where only the tough go)
- ☐ Forest (usually a place of natural solitude, occasionally a place where danger lurks)
- ☐ Jungle (usually an oppressive environment where primal forces rule)
- ☐ Mountain (does it symbolize some hierarchy in the story? Or a great revelation?)
- ☐ Plain (does the story concern freedom or equality? Is the society mundane?)
- ☐ River or road (both places that lead to adventures which test and teach the protagonist)

If events take place in a building, is the building a place of:
- ☐ comfort and refuge
- ☐ community and belonging
- ☐ isolation and loneliness
- ☐ anxiety and fear

Does the story take place:
- ☐ before a deadline or major event takes place (Does a deadline speed up the pace?)
- ☐ all in a single day (What makes that day special? Does someone make a change?)
- ☐ within a single season (Do events change a character or a situation permanently?)
- ☐ over a year (Does the mood of the story mirror the seasons? For instance, does everything seem dreary in winter and hopeful in spring?)

Does the author use settings to emphasize character differences, such as:
- ☐ the protagonist lives in a humble setting while the antagonist lives in a posh one (or vice versa)
- ☐ one lives in a loving community while the other lives in conflict or isolation
- ☐ the protagonist and antagonist live in competing communities

Structural Elements in Fiction: Autobiography/Biography/Memoir

Rating ☐

Title/Author _____

Was this book:
- ☐ an autobiography—a general account of a person's life by the same person
- ☐ a memoir—a brief account of a specific time or aspect of a person's life, by that person
- ☐ a biography—a general account of a person's life written by someone else

This book was written about or by a person who:
- ☐ was extraordinary in some way
- ☐ lived through extraordinary circumstances
- ☐ captured an ordinary life experience in an extraordinarily beautiful way

Did the book begin with:
- ☐ the birth of the individual
- ☐ a specific incident or time frame important to the person's later experiences

Which of the following did the book describe in detail:
- ☐ the setting (time or place) where the individual's experiences occurred
- ☐ the individual's relationships with other people
- ☐ the events in which the individual was involved
- ☐ the individual's experience of the events

Did the episodes related in the book seem to focus more on:
- ☐ the individual's participation in interesting events
- ☐ the individual's reflections about life in general
- ☐ lessons learned through specific events the individual experienced

Some of the episodes described:
- ☐ mistakes the individual made and learned from
- ☐ struggles the individual overcame by courage and persistence
- ☐ encounters in which other people provided encouragement at just the right time
- ☐ sacrifices the individual voluntarily made for the good of others

Did the book conclude with:
- ☐ the individual achieving a major goal or realizing a long-held hope
- ☐ the individual's newfound perspective or wisdom
- ☐ the individual's death or his or her lasting impact on the world

TEACHING INTERPRETATION

The worksheets in this section are designed to assist your student in thinking about how a work of fiction conveys meaning, both by grasping the unity of the plot and by considering how that unity comes about through various elements such as characters and scenes. Because not every work of fiction works in the same way—some create a theme through loosely related episodes, for instance, while others build to a clear and defining climax moment—not all of the worksheets apply to every book. By the time students are ready to work through the questions on these worksheets, they should also have the necessary knowledge to discern which type of worksheet applies to any literary work they have read in full.

Teaching Interpretation: Mystery or Action-packed Plot

Rating ☐

Title/Author _____

In the space provided or on another sheet of paper, briefly answer each question.

1. Describe the situation at the beginning of the novel.

2. What happens to shake things up?

3. What's at stake and for whom? Who stands to lose and gain by events?

4. What occurrences raise the stakes or increase the tension as the story progresses?

5. Does one character emerge as the likely hero?

6. What characteristics distinguish this character from the rest?

Appearance: _____

Abilities: _____

Values: _____

7. With whom do you think the author intends for you to empathize initially?

8. Does the author include any plot twists toward the end to change your mind?

9. Did you find the climax predictable? Surprising? Satisfying? Dull?

10. Do you think the author had a message to convey? If so, what was the message?

Handout: Teaching Interpretation through Character Webs and Values

In a novel with a simple plot and simplistic values (such as a mystery), conflicts are similarly simple. They usually look something like this:

Main Character → **opposes** ← **Villain or Organization**
(seeks truth and justice)   **(seeks to hide truth and evade justice)**

Example (from Arthur Conan Doyle's Adventures of Sherlock Holmes):

Sherlock Holmes → **opposes** ← **Professor Moriarty**
(seeks truth and justice)   **(seeks to hide truth and evade justice)**

In novel with more complicated but unified plots, authors often build character webs that put many characters into differing levels of conflict (Truby, 2007, p. 97). Remember, all conflict involves something that opposes the protagonist's true desire.

Example (from Jane Austen's *Pride and Prejudice*)

The protagonist, Lizzie, desires security for herself and for her family, but she insists on marrying with integrity (that is, for love)	opposes	Lydia, whose imprudent behavior ruins her own reputation and threatens Lizzie's and her sisters' chances to marry well
opposes		who opposes
Wickham, who purposefully represents himself as approachable and charming in order to deceive young ladies and misleads Lizzie about Darcy	who opposes	Darcy, whose high standards and higher position in the world lead him to disapprove of the Bennetts' foolish behaviors and act aloof, giving Lizze the false impression that he has improper pride and harbors many prejudices

Interpretation: Character Webs and Values

Rating ☐

Title/Author _____

Protagonist:	Secondary character
What the protagonist wants	How does this character keep the protagonist from succeeding?

opposes

who opposes	who opposes
Secondary character	Antagonist
How does this character confuse or upset the protagonist's goals?	How does the antagonist oppose the protagonist?

opposes

Interpretation: Character Webs and Values

In the space provided or on another sheet of paper, briefly answer each question.

1. What attributes, desires, and/or values do the protagonist and antagonist share?

2. What disputed object or misunderstanding holds the protagonist and antagonist in tension?

3. How do values differ between the protagonist and each secondary character?

4. How do values differ between the antagonist and each secondary character?

5. Do any secondary characters seem to present obstacles to the protagonist but effectively assist the protagonist in achieving his or her ultimate goals in the end?

6. Do any secondary characters intend to help the protagonist but ultimately impede the protagonist from achieving his or her goals?

7. How do the shared values between the protagonist and antagonist affect the outcome?

8. Based on the characters' values, what message or value(s) do you think the author wanted to convey through this story?

Interpretation: Thematic Works (such as Allegory, Fantasy, and Science Fiction)

Rating ☐

Title/Author _____

Many thematic works explore the question of good and evil. Identify ways the author exemplifies good and evil in the following categories. (Not all may apply.)

	Good	**Evil**
Characters		
Settings		
Symbols		
Actions		

1. What generalizations can you make about the good characters, settings, symbols, and actions? What values, attitudes, or beliefs do they reflect?

2. What generalizations can you make about bad characters?

3. If good prevails in the end, how? If evil prevails, why?

4. Do you think the author had a message to convey? If so, what was the message?

Interpretation: Episodic Novels

Rating ☐

Title/Author _____

1. How does the author unify the various episodes?
    ☐ Setting or story world

    ☐ Consistent character list

    ☐ The protagonist's desire

    ☐ An opposing force or conflict

2. Did the episodes involve the main character setting and achieving new goals, or did the main character learn some lesson from each episode?

3. Summarize two or three of the most important episodes. Why were these important?

4. Did any of the final episodes have significantly more impact than others? Which?

5. Can you identify a theme that is present in all (or most) of the episodes?

Teaching Interpretation: Coming-of-Age, Romance, or Psychological Novel

Rating ☐

Title/Author _____

In the space provided or on another sheet of paper, briefly answer each question.

1. What does the protagonist want/need/desire in the beginning of the novel?

2. Does the protagonist have a personal character flaw? If so, what is it?

3. Who or what is standing in the way of the protagonist getting what he or she wants?

4. How does the protagonist try to solve this problem or fill his or her need?

5. Does the protagonist have an epiphany that reveals the key to defeating the opposition or achieving the goal? If so, what is it?

6. Does the epiphany relate in any way to the protagonist's personal character flaw?

7. In the end, does the protagonist get what was desired in the beginning?

8. Based on this conclusion, what do you think is the author's message or theme?

Teaching Interpretation: The Protagonist's Desire and Ultimate Outcome

Rating ☐

Title/Author _____

Use the diagram below to consider potential themes and values in plays and novels.

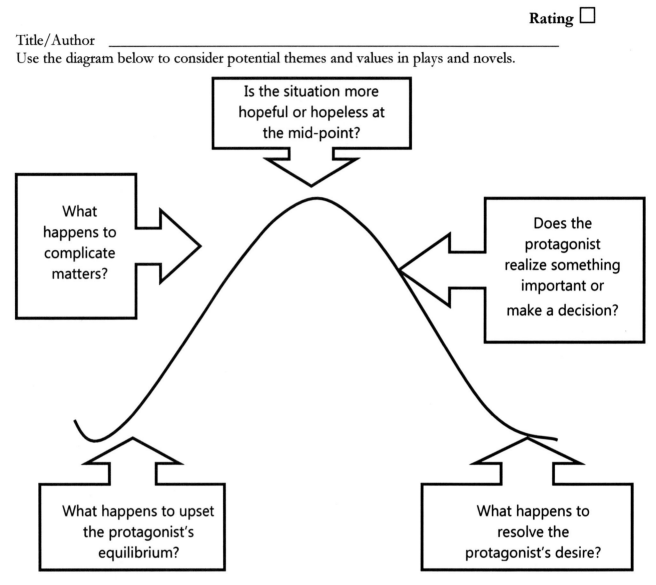

Is the situation more hopeful or hopeless at the mid-point?

What happens to complicate matters?

Does the protagonist realize something important or make a decision?

What happens to upset the protagonist's equilibrium?

What happens to resolve the protagonist's desire?

1. To what degree does the outcome of the novel correspond to the situation of the protagonist at the beginning? Does the protagonist get something he or she lacked at the beginning?

2. Does considering the contrasts between the situation at the beginning and the ultimate outcome as well as the state of affairs at the midpoint reveal a potential theme for the novel?

3. Is the outcome of events favorable or unfavorable to the protagonist in terms of his or her initial desire? What does the outcome reveal about the author's point of view about the theme?

HOW TO WRITE A BRIEF BOOK SUMMARY

When you write a summary, you capture the essence of a book in few words. Make sure to include the title and author of the book as well as basic information about the main character(s), setting, and plot. In a brief summary, you don't have to spell out all of the plot's twists and turns. Just name the specific activities that the main character does during the better part of the story and/or in the climax of the book. The key to brevity in a summary is to use specific and precise verbs. Here is an example of a summarizing statement that contains all of the essential components of a book summary:

> In Dr. Seuss's children's story, *How the Grinch Saved Christmas*, a disgruntled hermit plots to sabotage the holiday festivities of a local village, but later he repents and joins the community.

Notice how the verbs capture the essence of the story. The Grinch plots, repents, and joins. That's really the essence of the story, isn't it? Now, you might observe that this only condensed Dr. Seuss. So what, right? But watch how verbs capture the essence of this much longer (as in 1,000 pages long) work:

> In Margaret Mitchell's classic novel, *Gone with the Wind*, a vain and high-spirited Southern Belle craves attention and security even as she confronts challenges during and after the Civil War, but while Scarlett O'Hara manages to provide for her family in the wake of her family's financial ruin, she never learns to be content.

Could these summaries be longer? Absolutely! But notice how focusing on the protagonist and naming the protagonist's activities at the beginning, middle, and end of the book captures the essence of the story as concisely as possible.

Remember, concision is a quality you want to cultivate in your writing, and one place you especially want to be concise is when you write summary.

Let's look at how to concoct a brief summary of a literary work. Here's another summary that we will use as a model—something a little more complicated than the Grinch and a bit less complicated than Scarlett O'Hara.

> In Daphne Du Maurier's classic novel *Rebecca*, the unnamed protagonist marries Mr. Maxim de Winter, a wealthy widower whose former wife Rebecca died in a tragic accident. The new Mrs. De Winter feels daunted when she hears stories about Rebecca's beauty, charm, and social grace from her new neighbors. She even begins to suspect that her husband compares her to his former wife and worry that maybe he thinks he has made a mistake in marrying her. Only when Rebecca's body is found drowned in the bay does the protagonist find out the truth about Rebecca.

It's a good idea to begin your summary by naming the author, the type of literary work, and the title of the literary work. You can easily pack all of this information into an introductory phrase:

> In Daphne Du Maurier's classic novel *Rebecca*,

Next, name what the protagonist does to provide a context for the literary work:

> the unnamed protagonist marries Mr. Maxim de Winter, a wealthy widower whose former wife died in a tragic accident.

Once you have written the summarizing statement, the rest of the summary involves naming the specific actions the character takes during the first part of the book, the middle part of the book, and at the end of the story.

In the summary above, Mrs. De Winter ① feels daunted, ② begins to suspect and worry, ③ finds out the truth. Although each action of the main character is more complicated than that, those actions provide the framework for the summary. Sketching them out and adding details is not difficult. simply explain how or why the protagonist acts as he or she does at each point of the story.

LITERARY SUMMARY TEMPLATE

In _____'s _____,
　　　　　Author's name　　　　　　　　　　type of literary work

_____,
　　Title of the literary work (in italics or underline)

_____ _____
　　name the protagonist　　　　　　name the main activity of the main character

_____.
　　complete the sentence . . . .

In the beginning, _____ _____
　　　　　　　　　re-name the protagonist　　name the first main action of the character

_____
　　complete the sentence . . . .

_____.

Next, _____
　　　　　　　name what happens to complicate matters

_____
　　complete the sentence . . . .

_____.

But then, _____ _____
　　　　　re-name the protagonist　　name what the character does to resolve the problem

_____
　　complete the sentence . . . .

_____

_____.

In the end, _____ _____
　　　　　　re-name the protagonist　　　tell how matters resolve

_____
　　complete the sentence . . . .

_____

_____

_____.

LITERARY ANALYSES

A literary analysis is an essay in which students use evidence from one or more literary works to support a position or to explore an idea of their own. Vine and Faust (2000) find that writing deductively to support a position or writing inductively to explore an idea empowers students to make meaning out of texts (p. 107, 108). Whether students write to defend their ideas or to determine their ideas about a text does not matter so much as that students generate their own thinking about the text and that students support their thinking responsibly.

It would be very difficult (if not impossible) to suggest every way a student might legitimately write about literature, but in this section, I offer you two tools to help your student get started. The first is a list of questions and their implications to help students think about the kinds of questions that will help them bring to light their own ideas about a text. The second help I offer is a pair of literary analyses that I wrote myself; I include them so that students might get an idea of what a literary analysis might look like. Both essays include follow-up questions, challenging students to discern assertions I am making from the evidence I draw from outside sources or from the text to support my ideas.

HANDOUT FOR STUDENTS:

HOW TO DEVELOP YOUR OWN LITERARY ANALYSIS

How do you write a literary analysis? A literary analysis is basically your evaluation of a book based on what you got out of the book. When you first read books, you probably rated them based on your tastes alone, without being able to put your finger on what it was you liked. As you learn to understand how literature works, however, Mortimer Adler and Charles Van Doren suggest that your mature understanding will result in your evaluation of books becoming more analytical:

> You will say not only that you like or dislike the book, but also why. The reasons you give will, of course, have some critical relevance to the book itself, but in their first expression they are more likely to be about you— your preferences and prejudices—than about the book. Hence, to complete the task of criticism, you must objectify your reactions by pointing to those things in the book that caused them. You must pass from saying what you like or dislike and why, to saying what is good or bad about the book and why. (p. 214)

A FEW QUESTIONS YOU MIGHT EXPLORE IN YOUR LITERARY ANALYSIS:

What was the author trying to say with this literary work?

You might attempt to answer this question by exploring a theme you feel the author is grappling with or by exploring the author's juxtaposition of the protagonist's values versus those of the antagonist. You might also want to do a little research about the author's situation—was the author responding to a contemporary situation or a new philosophy? Such research can be as simple as looking up the author on Wikipedia. Of course, you might pursue further investigation if what you find there is sufficiently intriguing.

What techniques did the author use to accomplish a certain effect?

You might explore an author's use of figurative language, allusion, flashbacks or foreshadowing, or point-of-view for telling a story.

How does the work compare with another similar work?

You might explore similarities or differences between two books that struck you as particularly alike in some way.

How does the work reflect or challenge the values of society?

Many books are classic because they changed the way people thought. You might consider how a work like Sinclair's *The Jungle* challenged society at the time it was written; alternatively, you might explore how a classic work would challenge the values evident in our society, today.

How well did the author accomplish his or her purposes?

You might consider whether the work met the two criteria for successful fiction: whether or not it is believable, and whether or not it affects you emotionally.

Believability means that the characters, situation, and setting of the story do not get in the way of the reader's ability to get into the story. Notice here that believable does not mean plausible: even the imaginary characters and settings in works such as Tolkien's *The Lord of the Rings* feel believable because of their realistic depiction. Also, believability means that the reader feels as though the events in the story are plausible within the story world; they don't feel contrived by the author. For instance, I have noticed that some works of historical fiction feel implausible; they feel as though someone stuffed a bunch of characters and events into a particular historical timeframe primarily to educate me about that time, rather than because he or she had a real story to tell. I've also read books where I read a scene and felt like the author was deliberately attempting to advance his or her agenda through it. Such scenes preach rather than depict, and they strike me as contrived. I find that I usually don't like those books very well, even if I agree with the author's agenda. They simply don't strike me as believable fiction.

The other quality by which works of fiction are evaluated is whether they have the power to affect the reader: to make the reader feel something for or about the characters involved. Obviously, if a book bores you absolutely, it is not very successful, at least not with you. My five-star book rating almost always means a book has made me either laugh out loud or cry, and often both. For instance, when I read *All Quiet on the Western Front*, it made me laugh and cry at different points in the narrative. I rate the book highly because it affected me deeply.

TWO APPROACHES TO LITERARY ANALYSIS:

You can develop a literary analysis two different ways. One is to support an idea you have about a literary work with evidence from the text. With this approach, you'll need a clear thesis statement at the end of your introduction. Another approach is to explore something about a literary work that intrigues you, whether that's why a book captivated or irritated you, how an author achieved a certain effect, or what you think the book is trying to say.

To give you an idea of what a literary analysis might look like, I offer two examples of literary analyses. The first analysis follows a five-paragraph form and uses only summarized evidence from the text. The structure of this essay is fairly obvious: a reader can easily identify a thesis and three topic sentences. You should also be able to discern which sentences constitute my assertions and which contain evidence from the literary works in question. Evidence in the first analysis is entirely in summary form; there are no quotations from any actual text.

This second literary analysis is more complicated than the first: it represents my attempt to evaluate how well the author achieved one of his objectives, and it incorporates evidence from outside experts to help me achieve my task. This essay includes a number of characteristics you would expect to see in a college-level literary analysis: a more subtle thesis, infrequent topic sentences, evidence summarized and quoted from both the text in question and outside resources; and citations in the text and a bibliography at the end.

Literary Analysis 1

Whose Feet Matter Most:

What Austen's Novels Conclude about Romance

The adaptation of Jane's Austen's *Pride and Prejudice* in A&E's 1995 mini-series captured the romantic imaginations of women across the English-speaking world. What many people don't realize, however, is that Austen's novel was more than just a typical, girl-gets-boy in the end, happily-ever-after fairy-tale type of romance. Austen's novels, entertaining though they certainly are, were important entries in the then-active discussion about whether a woman should choose her own husband. At that time, wealth was largely inherited, so to whom a family's property would go was of supreme concern to a woman's relatives, especially her father. The romantic notions of the day, however, suggested that individuals should marry for love alone. In her novels, Austen explores the question of whether and to what degree romantic love should be the only criteria for marriage. The conclusion that seems to emerge in Austen's novels is that women can and should decide for themselves whom to marry, but that romance alone is not enough: Austen clearly thought that a woman's happiness depended on whether and how well a woman examined the character of her potential husband.

Traditionally, a woman's parents often decided whom she should marry, but Austen seemed to believe that most parents were not fit to make this decision for their daughters. In *Emma, Persuasion,* and *Sense and Sensibility,* Elinor, Emma, and Anne each have lost one parent and are left to care for the surviving parent. Of the men, Mr. Woodhouse seems feeble and worries constantly; Mr. Elliot, while no younger, is vain and self-absorbed. Mrs. Dashwood, on the other hand, seems to have little sense—she cannot understand her own finances nor does she see any reason to warn Marianne to beware Willoughby's excessive charm. In contrast, the heroines in *Pride and Prejudice, Northanger Abbey,* and *Mansfield Park* have living parents, but in each case, the parents are absent and unable to advise their daughters when crisis occurs. Although Austen's depiction of the Morlands is scant, Austen makes it clear that neither the Bennetts nor the Prices would have been likely to offer their daughters useful help: Fanny's father is a drunk and her mother is overwhelmed with the demands of running a busy household, while Mrs. Bennett is a social embarrassment and her husband, though clearly intelligent, has become cynical and careless as a result of putting up with his wife. Because he is intelligent, however, Austen takes care to reveal Mr. Bennett's neglect and lack of discernment in allowing Lydia to go away on a vacation, a decision that leads to disastrous results for the entire family.

In contrast, Austen's heroines all demonstrate wisdom in choosing husbands for themselves. After initially favoring Wickham, Lizzie gradually realizes Darcy's integrity. Emma, who attempts to make foolish matches for her friend, eventually realizes that she cannot live without Mr. Knightley. Anne Elliot turned down Captain Wentworth's first proposal on the counsel of her friend, but when time passes and other suitors fail to deter the couple's admiration for one another, Anne's wise choice eventually prevails. Austen's most courageous heroine, however, is Fanny Price, who withstands pressure from her uncle to marry Mr. Crawford, a man she believes to be more charming than virtuous, and she resists his persistent advances.

Although Austen clearly thinks women can and should choose their own husbands, she also warns women to take care in considering suitors, especially ones that are particularly charming or handsome. Willoughby, Crawford, and Wickham flatter women and behave deceptively, misrepresenting their motives or intentions. Willoughby admits to truly loving Marianne, but dumps her nonetheless because his aunt learns of his having "ruined" another woman and disinherits him, forcing him to marry for money rather than love. Although Crawford seems to reform to make himself agreeable to Fanny, in frustration he runs away and commits adultery with a married women, proving his untrustworthy character. Worst of all, Wickham seems to be an incurable cad who flirts constantly, tries but fails to ensnare a rich but naïve heiress, and must be bribed to marry Lydia after running away with her and ruining her reputation. Although Austen seems most concerned with men who are outwardly charming, she suggests that the prospect for future happiness is bleak also for women who marry men who are pretentious, vain, or vacuous. The best example here is probably Mr. Collins, Lizzie's obnoxious cousin, whom her friend Charlotte marries. Charlotte marries Mr. Collins for security rather than for love, and she confesses to Lizzie that she encourages her husband to spend the day in the garden: hardly a sign that Charlotte enjoys her husband's company.

What emerges is a position about how women should go about marriage: Austen rejects Charlotte's mildly mercenary marriage—and likely, this position was quite personal: Austen herself never married, although it is not improbable that an opportunity like Mr. Collins' proposal to Lizzie might have presented itself to her. But Austen also rejects the idea of letting passion get the better of a woman's sense, as Marianne learns and we suspect Lydia soon will. In a day and age when media continually portrays romance as finding a guy whose greatest characteristics are usually his six-pack abs, charm and wit, Austen's writings are not only delightful stories but a timely warning to women who want to be happy in their marriages. Happiness, she suggests, has little to do with how well a great guy sweeps you off your feet, girls, and everything to do with the integrity with which a true man stands on his.

Activity: using highlighters, identify the sentences indicated below.

1. Identify the thesis statement for this essay. The thesis statement tells you what the essay as a whole is about, and serves as a kind of map, telling you what each of the paragraphs that follow will be about.

2. Highlight the topic sentences in each body paragraph. Notice that each of these sentences contain my assertions about Austen's beliefs. If you read carefully, you should be able to find one more assertion hidden in one of the body paragraphs.

3. What assumptions do I make about my reader's familiarity with the works in question? What role does summary play in an analysis?

4. Highlight the sentences that contain supporting examples for assertions. Remember, examples should be specific enough for you to find if you were to crack open the book in question and look for them.

5. Highlight the reiteration of the thesis statement in the conclusion. How does it say the same thing as the thesis? How is it different?

6. Highlight the opening and concluding sentences of the essay. How do these sentences highlight the relevance of the literary work for my contemporary reader?

Literary Analysis 2

Haddon's Atypical Autistic:
An analysis of The Curious Incident of the Dog in the Night-time

In his book, *The Curious Incident of the Dog in the Night-time*, Mark Haddon depicts a fifteen-year-old autistic boy as a superbly logical detective sleuth who sets out to discover who killed the neighbor's dog with a garden fork, a mystery which ultimately leads him to discover the continued existence of the mother he previously thought dead. Although Haddon's portrayal of the character Christopher meets many criteria for autism, Haddon slightly misrepresents autism in a number of ways that are not immediately apparent upon a superficial reading but become more so upon analysis.

First, autism is typified by restricted interests, while Christopher's interests are quite diverse. This is not immediately apparent: one's first impression is that Christopher's interests are limited to mathematics, video games, and his pet rat, Toby. However, a closer reading reveals that this is hardly the case. Between action scenes, Haddon intersperses a number of flashbacks and parenthetical commentaries that reveal Christopher's knowledge of such disparate disciplines as astronomy, cardiology, Greek, geography, logic, literature, probability, Latin, chaos theory, theoretical physics, entomology and etymology. Considering the reduced curriculum taught in Christopher's school combined with the improbable depth of his father's library, one has to wonder where Christopher has been learning dead languages like Greek and Latin, not to mention theoretical physics. Christopher would have to be hyperlexic as well as savant in the areas of mathematical calculation, mapping, and drawing. Since only about 10% of autistic individuals demonstrate any savant abilities at all and significantly fewer autistic individuals demonstrate multiple savant abilities (Treffert, 2010), such an array of talents as Haddon's character possess, while not impossibly unrealistic, would be unlikely in the extreme.

The real difficulty, though, with the character of Christopher is that Haddon confuses the impaired social skills typically exhibited by individuals with autism with a complete lack of social affect. This is a subtle but important distinction. Haddon's portrayal reveals an absolute lack of affection even for Christopher's own parents, depicting Christopher as experiencing no grief upon learning that his mother had died (Haddon, 2003, p. 27), nor any gladness upon learning that she was still alive (p. 112), nor upon seeing her in person for the first time in years (p. 190). People to Christopher are merely sources of security or danger, and he transfers his father into the latter category upon learning that it was his father who killed the dog Wellington, upon which Christopher rejects his father's apology and pushes him away (p. 122). Although in individuals with autism, "normal stages of attachment are usually lacking"(Siegel, 1996, p. 33), observations of autistic children being separated from parents in a clinical setting reveal that "the autistic child *does* get comfort from the parent, but the comfort-seeking pattern is very atypical because it is so 'tuned down'" (Siegel, 1996, p. 34). Siegel emphasizes that individuals with autism do experience social attachment, or, to use a more common term, love.

Interestingly, Haddon's first person character never indicates any emotion nor initiates any affectionate behavior toward his father or anyone else. Instead, Christopher responds to his father's spread-out hand-touching ritual "because sometimes Father wants to give me a hug, but I do not like hugging people so we do this instead, and it means that he loves me" (Haddon, p. 16). But this explanation is backwards. Many if not most individuals with autism do feel affection and demonstrate affectionate behaviors; what distinguishes them from other individuals is not a lack of affectionate behavior but the way they go about it. One distinction is this regard is that the demonstration of affectionate behaviors often takes place without any eye-contact or talking; another is that "the autistic of PDD child tends to be the one who decides when it's time for a hug or a cuddle, and how long it will go on" (Siegel, p. 32). A more realistic portrayal of an individual with autism would have had Christopher ignore his father's requests for affection, but during moments of distress such as when he had been arrested, Christopher would have initiated the hand-touching ritual, not his father.

Of course, it is possible that Haddon intended to portray Christopher as an individual with autism who had been emotionally crippled by his family's dysfunction; however, I get the feeling that this is not the case. Haddon portrays Christopher as extraordinarily logical: in every incident Christopher behaves and emotes in ways most people would consider unfeeling, always because Christopher has come to a logical conclusion. Christopher rejects his father because he has concluded that his father can not be trusted. This conclusion causes Christopher to replace his former lack of emotion with fear.

Indeed, Haddon reduces Christopher's emotional capacity to the four primal emotions of rage, prey chase drive, fear, and curiosity/interest/anticipation—but in no instance does Christopher display any of the primary social emotions, which are sexual attraction, separation distress, social attachment, and play/roughhousing (Grandin, 2005, p. 93-94). These primary social emotions are not only common among humans, they are common among mammals. That the fifteen-year-old Christopher should be devoid of any of them is not typical of autism; it is not typical of any human being.

Grandin (2005), who has autism, indicates that it is not the lack of primary social emotions that identify individuals with autism, but the inability to experience ambiguity among such emotions. For instance, individuals with autism don't experience mixed emotions such as love-hate. "A child can be furious at his mom or dad one second, then completely forget about it the next," but "when a normal person" (that is, a person who doesn't have autism) "gets furiously angry with a person he loves, his brain hooks up anger and love and remembers it . . . his brain learns to have mixed emotions" (p. 90). According to Grandin, a distinguishing feature of people with autism is that they never experience this kind of ambiguity.

In her writing, Grandin repeatedly likens herself and other individuals with autism to young children and animals: "Emotionally, children are more like animals and autistic people . . . I think animals, children, and autistic people have simpler emotions because their brains have less ability to make connections, so their emotions stay more separate and compartmentalized" (p. 89) If I interpret Grandin correctly, a more realistic depiction of Christopher's reaction to his father's confession of murdering Wellington would not have been a purely logical conclusion and subsequent primal response of fear, but a momentary experience of rage which would almost immediately be overridden by social attachment. Yet Haddon depicts Christopher reacting with no sense of social attachment but only with the primal emotions of fear and rage.

Never does Haddon depict Christopher experiencing any of the primary social emotions of sexual attraction, separation distress (he does experience fear which kicks into fear-driven aggression when he runs away, but never does Christopher experience any sorrow or sense of loss at severing ties with either his father or Siobhan), social attachment, or play-roughhousing. In short, Christopher falls short of being quite human. Haddon, probably unwittingly, has created an autistic character who is in fact, an android—a character with some but not all of the characteristics of a human being.

That is not to say that I don't appreciate Haddon's achievement. Every author strives to create a unified work that can make readers laugh and cry at different points, so in terms of literary effectiveness, Haddon's novel is a success. And, in fact, Haddon does a particularly good job representing the impaired communication abilities of an individual with autism. Christopher's communication is consistently instrumental and never serves any expressive function. Furthermore, the author achieves a consistent voice with few variations in sentence form throughout. Read aloud, one's diction actually drones, atonally, much like an individual with autism (Siegel, p. 49). And this makes sense—one would expect that a linguistically gifted author would be most likely to accurately capture linguistic patterns.

That being said, *The Curious Incident of the Dog in the Night-time* does not portray the typical individual with autism and should not be considered instructive in this regard. Nor was instruction likely to have been Haddon's purpose in writing it. As the author of a work of fiction, Haddon purposes to entertain and affect readers, and he exaggerates his character's autistic savant abilities and social difficulties in order to do so. His depiction is realistic enough to be believable and therein lies its charm—and, if taken to be a definitive account of autism, therein lies its danger.

References

Grandin, T. & Johnson, C. (2005). Animals in translation: Using the mysteries of autism to decode animal behavior. USA: Simon & Schuster.

Haddon, M. (2003). The curious incident of the dog in the night-time. USA: Random House.

Siegel, B. (1996). The world of the autistic child: Understanding and treating autistic spectrum disorders. USA: Oxford University Press.

Treffert, D. (2010). The autistic savant. Wisconsin Medical Society. Retrieved from http://www.wisconsinmedicalsociety.org/savant_syndrome/savant_articles/autistic_savant

Activity: using highlighters, identify the information indicated below.

1. Use a highlighter to identify the thesis statement for this essay.

2. Highlight the topic sentences that specifically support the thesis statement in one color; highlight sentences that support other assertions in another color.

3. What assumptions do I make about my reader's familiarity with the works in question? What guidance do I give to help my reader locate my support in the original texts?

4. Highlight the sentences that contain supporting examples for assertions.

5. Highlight sentences containing support for my assertions from outside sources with another color.

5. Highlight the reiteration of the thesis statement in the conclusion with the same color you used to identify the thesis. How do these say the same thing? How are the two statements different?

6. Look at the opening sentences of the introduction. What function do these sentences serve?

7. Now consider the concluding sentences. Is the final evaluation of this book positive? Is it negative? How does the final sentence indicate the complexity of my final evaluation?

About the Author

Dena Luchsinger is a writer, a tutor, a lay minister and a homeschool teacher. A former licensed minister, she founded Proyecto Down, a non-profit, holistic ministry serving families affected by Down syndrome in Monterrey, Mexico. After returning stateside, she completed a Master of Arts degree with a dual emphasis in writing and practical theology; since then, she has been active in leading youth discussions in her local church, tutoring and teaching secondary students in writing English compositions, tutoring college writing students, and facilitating workshops for high school students and their parents. The parent of three children, one diagnosed with Down syndrome and autism, and another as "twice exceptional," or gifted and talented yet learning disabled, she is passionate about students of all ability levels achieving their potential. In addition to her publications through Crecer Publications, Dena Luchsinger is the author of two children's books: *Sometimes Smart is Good/A Veces es Bueno Ser Inteligente* (Eerdman's, 2007) and *Playing by the Rules: A Story about Autism* (Woodbine House, 2007).

CPSIA information can be obtained at www.ICGtesting.com
Printed in the USA
BVOW05s1130021013

332635BV00007B/88/P